Get Acquired

7 Steps to Your Most Lucrative Exit

ISBN: 9798873158591

Acknowledgements

Katy Ward (cover design)

Joon Han

Omeed Tabiei, Esq.

Stephen Resch

Axel Olson

Miguel Facussé

Stacey Crumrine

Josh Grillo

Table of Contents

Introduction

Honestly?

A lot of stuff in this book is going to get me into trouble.

It shares some dirty secrets about the business brokerage industry and about M&A (Mergers & Acquisitions) advisors.

However, it's also packed with insights I gained from personal mentors, conversations with experts, two decades of personal experience, and an insider's look into the workings of large companies that most people never see (both the good and the bad).

It's information that's usually kept hidden.
And there are plenty of people who want to keep it that way.

My perspective pisses some people off: when it comes to M&A, I say the more the merrier. I am spilling the beans of the industry in this book. In my opinion there's no point gatekeeping the information. Whoever has the grit to grow a business of their own should have access to useful resources to sell it.

In all the businesses I've had, I only used a business broker on my very first transaction, Cleanology. You'll see stories in here about how that transaction went down.

But after that experience, by the time I'd started my next business, I was ready to skip the middleman and sell it on my own this time.

I thought to myself:
"I built this company from the ground up. I did the marketing and sales, I grew the revenue, and know this business like the back of my hand, so I should be able to sell it myself, right?"

I did a quick search to make sure there was no law or rule against it. And sure enough, similar to "For Sale By Owner" in real estate, there's no requirement to have a business broker. People use them because they don't know how this process works, which is completely fair. But if you can bypass them and go straight to the knowledge, even better. Please promise to report back if you use this book to do the same.

Successfully exiting a business is a major accomplishment. Doing this without the assistance of an advisor or broker?

That's a next-level achievement. Plus, selling on your own saves the fees/commissions you would otherwise be paying out to them.

Exits are such a big deal because **only the dedicated few make it this far in the first place.** If you're reading this, you're in the minority of the population who doesn't just *want* to be an entrepreneur, but actually *is* one.

It feels like everyone and anyone is calling themselves an 'entrepreneur' these days. Anyone with internet access can start a business. No startup costs, no rent, no need for employees. The barrier to entry is... wait, there is *no* barrier to entry now.

Who can blame them? Startup culture is sexy, enticing, and full of unicorns with too many zeros behind their valuation. Right?

Well, remember that about 90% of startups fail.

This stat is widely debated, but after my first couple of successful exits, in different industries, from house cleaning and Christmas trees to wellness, luxury car rentals, real estate, and tech – I realized most business owners weren't getting the same results. They weren't all selling each venture and moving to the next.

That's why I decided to write this book: to teach you that you can (and should) sell your business. And you can do it on your own if you want. You'll be hearing things I've never discussed publicly, not even on any podcast interviews.

I'll also share some stories about the companies we get to dig deep into while taking them to market.

Sure, my M&A firm, The Magnolia Firm, has a white-glove process to get sellers their dream outcome, but it's not accessible to everyone. I can confidently say that we're one of the best, locking in the best terms and above-average multiples for our sellers.

My Why:
Primarily, I wanted to publish this book for small businesses under $1 million in asking price, because most times, it's hard to find someone to represent them.

That purchase price is considered too small for most advisors and brokers to take. We're all a little out of touch in this industry labeling that number as small, but for a business owner that's a lot of money. It can change someone's life and set them up for security. I've been there. Or maybe you don't need it, but you deserve it because you've built a business that commands that value.

Unfortunately, these businesses under $1M in asking price often just close down because the thought of trying to sell their own company is too confusing, or they don't even know they can sell their business.

So here's the step-by-step guide on how to sell your company – *everything*.

I've read other books about "How to Sell Your Company." Most business brokers write books like this to gatekeep information and intentionally overcomplicate the process. **Don't fall for it.**

Could this be because they want you to hire their firm to handle the transaction?
Unfortunately, yes.

The goal of this book is to simplify the process into action steps that you can take on your own (if you want to).

Actually, this might be one of the only books out there from a brokerage firm that is **transparently telling you: brokers aren't necessary**. Don't let any broker tell you that you can't do it yourself.

On top of it all, **most people don't know** that there is not a specific license for business brokers the same way there is in real estate. This is especially true when it comes to selling remote businesses because there isn't negotiation of commercial real estate leases. It's actually a pretty unregulated industry, which can be concerning – makes it easier for inexperienced brokers to take advantage of founders who are itching to sell. In some states a real estate license is needed to practice (luckily, I've had a license since 2001 even though I was not actively using mine for over two decades).

I could not believe that this was all I needed to become a business broker. *Really*? Selling a business is nothing like selling a house. It is incredibly nuanced, has so many moving parts, and is hard to run comps because there's no public data on previous sales the way there is for properties.

Because the space is so dependent on experience, I think it should be mandatory for brokers to have built and ideally exited their own company before entering this industry.

If you haven't had your first exit, you can still do it yourself.

That's what this book is for. It will arm you with everything you need to handle your own transaction – or at least give you the knowledge to work with a broker or intermediary without getting pushed around. If you do decide to go this route, be sure to use our handy "Questions to ask a Broker before signing with them" guide that is on our free resources page. I'm sure they aren't pleased with me for putting this together, because it gives you the opportunity to grill them and push past some of their bluffs, but someone needed to.

However, I am confident that you can do it on your own.

Why am I so sure? Here's my story.

It All Started With $1,000

Yep, just $1K. Here's how.

My hero is Richard Branson. I'd been a fan of his since the early 2000's. His ability to blend business acumen with genuine kindness has always struck a chord. So, when I decided that I wanted to meet him, it felt like setting my sights on the stars.

That goal seemed almost too unreasonable to admit out loud. *Almost.*

Picture me back in 2013: a scrappy entrepreneur just planting the seeds of what would become a thriving business. I was still learning the ropes, fueled by passion rather than experience. That was when I heard Richard would be in San Diego for a movie premiere. Opportunity had knocked, and I was ready to answer.

At the end of him speaking that day, I ran up on stage and handed him a check for a thousand dollars to his charity, Virgin Unite, then quickly ran off. I knew it wasn't much compared to the six and seven figure donations Virgin Unite usually gets from generous donors, but it was a lot for me at the time. I gave it with no expectations of where it would lead.

To my astonishment, within an hour, Richard Branson himself called to thank me. That call – his voice on the other end – it was surreal. He was so gracious. I could not believe it for that small of a check. I immediately offered free massages at my spa to him and his wife, but he said he was flying out in a few hours.

That conversation sparked something in me, and I spent the next few years building *hard*.

Fast forward to 2017. I had just sold the spa, Eco Chateau. The journey had been a rollercoaster of highs and lows, but I came out stronger, wiser, and, thankfully, more financially secure.

I was able to get in touch with Richard by email, reminding

him of our story with the $1,000 check. I said I had another check for Virgin Unite, but this time with some extra zeros. My only request was that I hand it to him in person, no hidden agenda.

He invited me out to Paris and offered to meet me for breakfast. Wow. He was humble, engaging, and incredibly insightful. We talked about everything from cryptocurrency, going to space with Virgin Galactic, to the power of meditation.

Richard later wrote a blog post about this story and shared it on his social media platforms about a month later. I didn't even realize he'd done this until my friends reached out to me who had seen it. That meant the world to me. It wasn't just the recognition; it was a validation of my journey and our shared passion for entrepreneurship. It was then that I remembered he'd taken notes on a pad during our breakfast in Paris to reflect on and write about later. I was touched.

So when I published my first book in 2018 (about the growing shared housing market), naturally he was the first person I thought of to write the foreword. To my surprise and delight, he agreed. I'll insert it here.

Foreword

As someone who has worked tirelessly to build a brand worth being proud of, I'm no stranger to the feeling of fierce motivation and passion for a vision. This core ambition is something I share with Christine, with whom I was able to personally spend time with and explore these ideas together. She told me about the innovative ways in which she hopes to reimagine living spaces and create a sense of comradery, luxury and efficiency by sharing resources throughout these homes with her current venture, Kindred Quarters. Christine is someone who works tirelessly on giving back and helping others. It's refreshing to be around such a passionate and talented entrepreneur working on making this world a better place.

As a serial entrepreneur, she has already made some fantastic strides with eight successful companies under her belt. Her experience and ambition have allowed her to think outside the box and refuse to back down. I was fascinated by her commitment to turn the real estate industry on its head and develop solutions to a widespread problem as opposed to mere ways of coping. Instead of accepting that housing is becoming scarce in space and increasingly costly, she decided to create an answer that solves multiple pains at once. These core elements of community and sharing of resources are not only key to a fulfilling life, but also to any thriving business.

For these reasons, I'm delighted to introduce the content you're about to dive into. When a seemingly impossible challenge presents itself, I am a proponent of always pushing harder and reaffirming the commitment to succeed. The harder a problem appears, the more exciting it will be to solve. That's why the fantastic tools you're about to learn will serve you in countless corners of your life. So prepare to view things in a new way, because once you take these ideas in, there's no turning back.

-Richard Branson

My next goal? To add another zero with a $1M donation. And with every client the firm helps, every business we sell, we're inching closer to it.

I share all of this because it's why I'm writing this book now: Selling my own business **changed my life.** It's what gave me the ability to live the way I wanted.

Everyone has a different definition of success. For me personally, it's *__freedom:__* Freedom to do what I want, where I want, with who I want. Other than my very first exit (I'll share that story) I didn't have a broker – I did it by myself. And if I can do it, so can you.

But this time, you have a major advantage that I didn't: you have this book as a guide with all the steps that I learned through trial and error.

By sharing the ungated tools in this book to do it all on your own, my hope is that you can experience whatever an abundant life looks like to you.

Chapter 1:
How Exits Make Millionaires (and can make you one too)

"I find that the harder I work, the more luck I seem to have." - Thomas Jefferson

---

Some of the "my first million" journeys start with a vision quest. Some start at an Ivy League university. Others start at rock bottom.

It was 2003. I was 23 years old with $45,000 in credit card debt. By my calculations, a traditional job wasn't going to be enough to get me out of the hole.

I wanted to start a business but had no money to get it off the ground. But I was willing to do anything.

So I did:

I charged $300 worth of cleaning supplies onto my last maxed-out credit card (yes you can laugh) and started cleaning apartments in Downtown San Diego. This was 2003 when the new Petco Stadium opened and new highrises were starting to rapidly grow our skyline.

I had no idea how to even clean properly, so I hired a few ladies to help me out – who only spoke Spanish by the way, so I learned in real time to keep up.

There I was: cleaning homes all day and bartending nights to cover personal and business expenses. I did this for about 2 years until I could afford a tiny office and transitioned from cleaner to manager. I was breathing above water now, but not thriving.

I realized that, for my business to perform infinitely better, the responsibility was up to me. I looked at my competitors to see what the industry was missing: most cleaning companies at the time were challenging to communicate with, lacked a coordinator proficient in English, and weren't eco-friendly, which is important to a lot of customers. Recognizing this gap in the market, I moved in to fill it. I also made one of the best decisions by changing the company name from Christine's Cleaning Service to Cleanology.

Soon, we became the largest privately-owned cleaning company serving all of San Diego. I was approached to franchise nationally, but I was ready to move on and ultimately decided to sell for a six-figure amount. I had no idea how to sell my company, so I reached out to local brokers for assistance. They turned out to be rude and condescending (but joke's on them – little do they know they provided perfect material for my 'Broker Bob' comedy shorts on The Magnolia Firm's social channels where I poke fun at outdated brokers like them).

In the end I worked with a 'decent' broker. I say decent because there were a few red flags that came up for me during the transaction.

- First, he tried to pressure me to take an offer that was $50,000 less than my asking price. Sometimes this is worth entertaining, but I could tell that he just wanted to quickly close the deal to get his commission check. I was in my 20's back then, but still skeptical enough to call him out on it. It was a $50,000 loss for me but only a $5,000 loss on his commission. As much as it frustrated him, I stayed true to my asking price.

- Secondly, he called me to present a lowball offer. I passed. He pushed back, saying he would fax (yes, fax machines back then) the written offer over. He told me I had to look at it and check off whether I was declining the offer. I said I would not waste my time doing that.

  But guess what? That same buyer ended up paying full price for my business. Yep, the one that initially came in at an insultingly low price. You never know how things will unfold – but please don't let someone lowball you, that's the game of negotiating (a game that I live for).

- Third thing was a big one that is burned into my brain to this day: he wrote in the agreement that I would do *way more* training than acceptable. This is one of the reasons I make sure my sellers do not make the same mistake.

  We will cover more about training in Chapter 7, but I know stories are easier to remember, so let me tell you the biggest learning lesson and shock that was made during this transaction.

  In the templated purchase agreement my broker provided, it had a default training period provision of three months. I caught it and told him it would not take three full months to train the new owner. It had management in place, a great team of over 35 employees, and I only worked about 5-10 hours a week. Plus, I had already started my next company, a social media firm. I didn't have the time to commit 3 full months to train the new owner (unpaid).

This all happened in May 2010, but I remember it like it was yesterday. He told me: "Christine, the buyer will *never* take you up on that much time for training, he will only take about 2 weeks of your time, at most. We add that into the agreement because buyers like to see it."

You guessed it. The buyer used every minute of that training provision. For three months I was there because "that's what was in the contract". I didn't have a choice – I'd trusted my broker and should have stuck with my gut.

But now I can see the positive because it made me a stickler for this stuff. For our clients, we make it very clear in both the LOI (Letter of Intent) and the Purchase Agreement how much time needs to be committed to training and handoff of the business. Please don't forget this when you are running your own transaction. Offer the actual time you believe it will take to fully train, onboard, handoff clients, get a handle on managing the team, and set them up for success. If you already have managers in place and a turnkey business where you only work about 10 hours a week, then usually a total of 60 hours, to be used within 3 months, is very appropriate. It's also nice to include in the agreement that you can be hired anytime in the future as an hourly consultant at a rate of "x". Standard is typically anywhere from $75/hr to $250/hr.

Regardless, the satisfaction of selling my business for a lump sum gave me so much enthusiasm. I was hooked. I wanted to do it again: start more businesses, grow them, and sell them (and that's exactly what I did).

This book is going to print in December 2023, marking my 20-year anniversary of becoming an entrepreneur by starting Cleanology.

It didn't hit me that I should start helping others sell their companies until the fall of 2021: I was in a monthly mastermind group with a bunch of fellow business owners who started venting about their challenges trying to sell their businesses. They were so over it. One had spent $25K with a broker and gotten nothing in return. Another had tested multiple brokers, each worse than the next, and another was charged so much for the sale that they'd walk away with barely any profit. I couldn't help but I knew there had to be a better way to help these people. And behold, The Magnolia Firm was born.

Now, in this current phase of life, I've officially moved to the other side of the table: helping fellow entrepreneurs have this experience. I didn't realize that all those ventures, failures, negotiations, and sales were setting me up to do it on behalf of others. This book brings it all together.

> **There's debate over the exact percentage, but studies have found that 70-80% of millionaires are 'self-made'. How did these self-made millionaires get there? For at least half, it's entrepreneurship.**
>
> **Almost all billionaires get there by owning businesses (or at least a stake in them, like Warren Buffet). This is because business ownership creates uncapped financial leverage – paving the way to massive net worth.**

Growing and selling a company is one of the most effective pathways to wealth. But here's more reasons why it's worth it:

- *Financial Freedom*
  - One of the most obvious benefits – the impact of cashing out of your business at the right time can be life-changing. Some founders want to use the funds to retire (if it's a big enough check, never work again), take a few years off and travel, buy property, invest, the list goes on.
- *Career Freedom*
  - Another major driver for founders to sell is that they only have so much capacity, and this business isn't sparking joy anymore. Nobody can do everything all at once. Maybe it's just fatigue, a lack or passion, or a new venture on the horizon that they know needs to take priority.
- *Lifestyle Freedom*
  - Many founders want to exit because it frees up their time – something that can't be replaced. The life of a founder is gritty and satisfying, but it can lack balance. Your business is your baby. But some founders enter another phase of life where they want different things to take priority, like their family.
- *Mental Freedom*
  - And of course, this one is the least tangible but can be the most powerful: owners are just plain tired. And when they're done, they're done.

Burnout is a real thing, and you can't put a price on a healthy mental/emotional state. *Note: Try to exit before this gets intense for you. Sellers get so "over it" that they stop growing the business and settle for lowball offers because they're itching to get out.

And the final reason.... we can't forget about the clout, which is just a cherry-on-top. It just feels good to have an exit under your belt and to share that achievement with others, because it's a massive accomplishment that puts you in the upper echelon of entrepreneurs.

Also, it makes it that much easier to raise capital in your future ventures, especially if you want to go big on your next one.

Another reason to sell your business right now: timing.
Acquisitions are sexier than ever.

Translation: they are actually profitable (yes startups, we're looking at you).

You've seen all the gurus and influencers charging thousands for their courses on "How to acquire a company with zero down" or "Replace your corporate income by acquiring laundromats or car washes". And for some people this works out. For others, they're tied to a physical business with the liability of machines breaking, utilities rising, churning employees, and dealing with a customer LTV of maybe $1200, on the high side. These cap out quickly and are tough to scale.

However, profitable business acquisitions, especially in the technology sector, are a sellers' market.
This is great news for you.

But it didn't happen overnight:
In 2021 we saw a ton of fallout and layoffs in the startup world. The bubble burst. It became harder for startups to raise capital on valuations that weren't manifesting in real performance.

The era of "normalizing" being in the red for several years had come to an end. Nowadays, we see so many people wanting to skip the startup phase and acquire an established profitable business – and they're willing to pay for it. This puts you in a great position as a business owner because you have what they want.

For you to achieve your dream exit, one that gives you all your desired outcomes, it'll depend on how well you follow the steps we're about to cover in the coming chapters. We'll take you chronologically through each stage of selling in the real order that they happen. It's the exact process my firm follows to generate tens of millions of dollars in exits.

If you implement them to the fullest extent, I promise your sale will reflect that.

Chapter 2:
Start From the End (how to reverse-engineer your exit)

"This is mile 23 of a marathon and you are going to sprint the last 3 miles." – Christine McDannell

---

Sad truth: Most exits are destined for a below-average sale the second they hit the market.

Why?
Because the majority of owners just decide to list it one day to 'test the waters'. This is actually the worst thing you can do.

> **The *best* thing you can do is prepare for your exit *before* the business ever goes live on the market. This preparation process can have a major positive impact on your final sale price.**

Exit-planned acquisitions are so game-changing because they allow the owner (you) to define your ideal exit and then work backwards, reverse-engineering that outcome to make it possible.

Most business owners wind up with an underwhelming acquisition price (or no sale at all) because **there's a gap between what they think their business is worth and where it's actually at**. They either don't realize that the gap exists, because they don't understand the true value of their business, *OR* they have no idea how to get there, so they settle for less (or sometimes nothing at all).

Here's a quick story:

Me and my friend Sarah were at a brunch in the fall of 2021. I was telling her about a transaction I was just completing for another friend of mine. After hearing this, she mentioned she was gearing up to shut down the marketing firm she had for 20 years. She said it was not worth anything. I was shocked – this wasn't my first time hearing about her company, and I knew it worked with big brands as clients. It was hard for me to believe it was worthless.

Sarah said she was too busy with her new role at a tech startup, while being a single mom, that she just didn't want to worry about selling it. She wanted to get it off her plate and walk.

But in that chat I learned a few things about her company: how many team members it had, her current revenue and profit, how significantly the revenue was declining, and that her key team member was about to depart on maternity leave in a few months.

Plenty of points could be considered an elephant in the room (always important for you to disclose these to buyers upfront). I told her it couldn't hurt to at least take it to market just to see if we can get her something for it. She walked away with a multiple 6-figure sale.

The point of the story is that a lot of times the business owner is so in the weeds, frustrated, and overwhelmed that they can't see all the value in their business. I don't want this to be you.

The Mistake of the Masses

Here's the classic downward spiral of an un-strategized exit (I've seen it too much, and it's heartbreaking every single time):

- The business owner is getting tired of running their business. They want to cash out, move on to something new, relax, pivot. They're already feeling the discomfort of being tied to it. One day they crack under the frustration and think "Ok, I'll just list it for sale and see if I get any bites. It can't hurt, right?"

- Because this is a discomfort-driven decision, they haven't done the work to learn the exact value of their current business. They think there's no harm aiming high, on the off chance that someone bites.

- Some inquiries might come in, but the time that it takes talking to each lead is eating into the hours that the owner would spend running it and ideally *growing* the business to make the sale possible.

- Now there's another compounding issue because the owner was over their business to begin with, and now they're more overloaded than ever juggling the leads with trying to keep the company healthy to reflect the price they're asking.

- It's too much. The owner is physically exhausted and emotionally over the business, so its numbers are trending down, which means leads are drying up. It's been sitting on the market for a while now, making buyers skeptical about the quality.

- At this point, one of two things tend to happen: (1) a lowball offer comes in so the owner just decides to cut their losses and take it, or (2) nothing happens so the business slowly dies / they pull the plug and walk away.

Since you're reading this, that story doesn't have to be you.

Our job is to help you bridge the gap between your *dream number* and the *real number* that you get.

Wrong Way (most biz owners)	*Right Way (you)*
- Feels burned out running their business – hits a breaking point where they're "over it" and lists the company for sale - Wants a certain price for their business but can't prove the value to a buyer - Thinks it's harmless to test the market by	- Plans their exit *in advance* – before they're burned out (this allows them to approach it from a place of abundance instead of scarcity or need) - Wants a certain price for their business, knows what it's accurately worth now, and recognizes that

<table>
<tr>
<td>

listing it publicly at their 'dream price'

- Gets burned out while the listing sits on the market, so the business suffers, making it harder to sell

- Takes a low offer or stops the business altogether

</td>
<td>

steps are needed to connect them

- Gameplans and implements the steps to reach the EBITDA that gets them to that ideal price

- Lists it for sale when the business supports their goal price (and buyers agree)

</td>
</tr>
</table>

How Do I Know When it's Time to Sell?

A good rule of thumb is to start preparing your business when you feel *interested in / open to selling* down the road, but don't feel urgency yet.

Why?

You never want to sell when you're driven by pain / discomfort to get rid of it.

Most business owners already make a critical mistake here: they're ready to give up before the exhausting journey of selling begins. That's why it's important to start planning the exit *before* you get burned out of the business, so you have time to get it to the selling point you want.

Even with my own company it wasn't something that crossed my mind. It's not necessarily when you hit a specific revenue point or net income. It's usually when the business is running so smoothly that it doesn't need you anymore.

Like the quote at the beginning of the chapter, remember: *this is mile 23 of a marathon and you are going to* **sprint** *the last 3 miles.*

Listen, I understand the burnout. We will cover 'Deal Fatigue' later in the book (that is real). However, it can be really hard to keep your enthusiasm up, your drive, your willingness to continue growing the company. You might be over it already and have one foot out the door.

Here are some of the triggers that can push a business owner over the edge:
- An employee did not show up
- An unhappy client has a meltdown
- Someone threatens a lawsuit
- Payroll feel like a struggle because cash flow is lumpy

This is usually the moment when someone is contemplating exiting their company.

Many of our clients come to us ready to take *anything* for their business – they're just ready to be done. A recent client was prepared to literally just give the company to one of her employees, and didn't realize selling it was a viable option. It almost always is.

But selling your company for the ideal price isn't a stroke of luck, it's the result of months / years of planning behind the scenes up to that point.

A great place to start is by getting ultra-clear on your financial goals – not your business ones, your personal ones. Here's why:

'Want' Number vs. 'Need' Number

Most owners have a dream price for their business.

But instead, I encourage you to calculate a real number that you need to sell it at to reach the outcomes that are most important to you. For example:

- Many owners are selling for the goal of financial freedom. If you're one of them, you need to calculate what amount of money will allow you to reach that.
  - *Example:* One of our recent sellers decided to exit. He **wanted** $3 Million in his pocket – and

he picked this number based on his personal goal to pull 5% in distributions per year to live comfortably, without having to work again. The price point was more important to him than the urgency of selling immediately, so he was comfortable taking several months to grow the business and put operators in place to get to the dream sale number.

- Other owners **need** a certain number at minimum to break even before money goes into their pocket.
  - *Example:* An imaginary founder, let's call him Joe, **needs** $1 Million to pay off outstanding business debt, shareholders, and investors so he can move on to the next project without clearing those debts out of pocket. Any less than this $1M means he wouldn't break even. To zero those out completely, he has to keep in mind that taxes must be paid on the income of selling the business, so a $1M sale price wouldn't be enough.

This practice helps you establish your upper and lower price points.

The Right Buyer: What to Look For

Some ideal buyer traits are universal, and others will be unique to your business. This goes far beyond having the funds to make the purchase. Here's the baseline of what a buyer should have:

- *Industry Knowledge:*
  A strong buyer should be competent in the industry your business operates in *or* have the skillset to put someone in place that will be owning the operations.

- *Strategic Fit:*
  Look for a buyer who has the ability to grow your business – not just maintain it as-is, and definitely not someone who will let it decline. It's common that sellers will hand off their business to the highest bidder but they know deep down that person will run it into the ground. It's not worth it. They should have the desire and capacity to expand the company's operations or enter new markets.

- *Financial Capacity:*
  On the flip side, you might encounter a buyer who seems like a great fit with their passion and experience, but just doesn't have the funds to acquire. Of course, there are a ton of creative financing options, and we will go over that in detail later in this book since sellers take on risk in most of the alternative options.

- *Cultural Alignment:*
  Another massive factor that sellers overlook is the culture fit. A buyer might tick all of the boxes but just doesn't mesh well with the brand or team - this is a real thing. Look for a buyer whose values align with your

company's culture to ensure that the employees and customers thrive – which in turn makes the business thrive.

Let's Define Your Perfect Sale

Aside from universally positive buyer traits above, there are also specific ones that will make a buyer just right for *your business*. To do this, you need to define who they are in excruciating detail. It seems excessive, but trust me, it works.

Who is going to buy your business? What are their priorities? What will the sale look like? By defining this, you could get the company sold *without ever having to list it on the open market* – that's the power of this exercise.

Exercise: Dream Sale Mapping

This is the Dream Sale exercise that I have sellers go through. This is going to be your roadmap to the finish line (Click the QR code at the end of this chapter to download for free)

- Get into a comfortable relaxed state. Get out of your current reality and into the imagined future. Consider: *Exactly what does my dream life look like for me? Where am I right now in relation to it?*
- Next: *How does selling my business get me closer to this reality?*
- Now write down the exact date that you would love to

have your business sold by. Write it in past tense how the sale went down, almost like a mini press release. Once you do this, you are putting it out there to unfold.

- Write down the key qualities you *know* you want your buyer to have. Write down the things you do *not* want to compromise on, so you can look back here as your north star.

- I also recommend doing the Dream Buyer exercise to identify the ideal *buyer* for your business. Many buyers who have done this exercise realize that they already know someone who would be perfect, or it helps them better identify the right fit when it comes along.

TIP:

I **highly recommend** you do the Dream Sale mapping and tape it to the wall where you work every day to keep it top of mind. **You can click the QR code** at the end of this chapter to download for free) There's something about doing it on paper that resonates harder.

Conduct a Gap Analysis

Now that you know what you want, you need to see how far it is from where you are now. A Gap Analysis is a great way to identify the space between where your business is *currently* and where you *want* it to be. It compares the two and identifies the steps to bridge the gap.

Forbes makes a helpful template for this, but here's a helpful overview of how to approach it:

1. *Identify the current situation.*
   Define where you're at now.
2. *Set S.M.A.R.T goals of where you want to end up.*
   These goals should be specific, measurable, achievable, relevant, and time-bound. The more specific the better.
3. *Assess the gaps between where you are & where you want to be.*
   What's the distance between the current stage and the specific desired one? What needs to happen to get there? What are the potential blockers?
4. *Break down a plan to close existing gaps.*
   Now that you've identified the issues and desired outcome, it's time to solve them. What are the action items that bridge the gaps between you and your end goals? Does it involve hiring, increasing client lifetime value, closing an extra 2 clients per month?

Assemble Your Advisors

One of the toughest parts about selling is the overwhelm of opinions coming at you from the outside. It's understandable

– you haven't done this before and want plenty of input to fill your knowledge gaps. That's normal.

Keep in mind that everyone is going to have recommendations on what you should do – most of them influenced by their own personal experiences and bias. If you listen to all of them, you'll be back at square one, more confused than ever (or worse, take bad advice that damages your deal).

Just be careful about crowdsourcing advice – especially when talking to someone with a personal stake in your deal, like brokers or service providers who want to earn your business. They may use scare tactics to sway you (or butter you up).

However, high quality advisors and resources can get you to an outcome that was never possible on your own. They can bridge the gap we talked about more easily.

Yes, sometimes they come with a fee, but that can pay for itself many times over with the value added. Some charge a percentage of the deal, others bill hourly, and others are flat rate by scope. The right choice for you will depend on how involved you want them to be and how comfortable you are handing off responsibilities.

Here's the basic advisory roles to consider bringing on.

TIP:

When it comes time to sell your company, get these specialists lined up (your *"Three Wise Men"* or women):

1. A strong **accountant**

   How they'll help:
   - *Before* – get your P&Ls in order
   - *During* – helping with tax planning
   - *After* – properly categorize the income

2. A strong **lawyer**

   How they'll help:
   - Review transaction documents like the LOI and Purchase Agreement

Note: Go for an M&A lawyer who understands the process. Many lawyers, even those specializing in M&A, play a role in deals falling apart because they can hyperfocus on minutia and are naturally looking for ways the deal could *not* work. To be fair, that's part of their job. (After all, they're billed hourly to look for any possible holes, so their motivation is different from the buyer/seller who *wants* the deal to work out).

> 3. *Optional:* A strong **Intermediary or M&A Advisor** (aka Business Broker)
>
> How they'll help:
>
> - Manage the deal to the finish line (or skip this and do it alone). Make sure they aren't outdated or unethical; a misguided choice can do more harm than good. A competent intermediary, however, can make all the difference.
> - Interface between both parties to find common ground and propel the deal forward.
>
> Depending on the size of your business, additional experts can be useful, but you can get pretty far into high 7-figure deals with just these key people. Keep it lean when you can.

A common question: What's the difference between a **business broker**, an **M&A advisor**, and a **business intermediary**? Is there a difference?

You will see all three being used interchangeably; however, there's a difference in my opinion.

- It's one of the reasons I don't usually call myself or anyone at The Magnolia Firm a **"business broker."**

They have a horrible reputation and are close to car salesmen in that they just want to get their cut by selling the company quickly, as opposed to fighting for the best interest of their client. I honestly despise this title and never use it for myself.

- As for "**intermediary**," here is Webster's Definition: "One that acts as a means or go-between in a matter involving other parties." In about 90% of our transactions, the buyer does not have a broker or intermediary on their side, so intermediary is a more accurate title. They work hard to act in everyone's good faith to create a win-win for all parties involved.
- Lastly, "**M&A advisor**." I also use this sometimes. This tends to apply to larger deals where the seller is being acquired or merging with another firm. These deals are complicated to pull off, but really rewarding to get to the finish line in my opinion.

Reinforce Your Team Members

When someone buys your business, it's not just the brand they see the value in – it's the client base, the systems, and **the team you've built.**

One of the biggest reasons a buyer acquires your company is for the operations and team members. Unfortunately, some owners are so involved and interconnected with their team that they haven't created systematic, repeatable processes. Don't let this be you. A business that needs you isn't a flex, it's a disadvantage.

Make sure you have detailed **SOPs** (Standard Operating Procedures) breaking down how every single process of the business runs, in writing. It's like your business playbook; it's the bible. The goal of this resource is that a new employee could come in and get up to speed effectively with just this resource. Ideally, it should be so digestible that even a 12-year-old could follow along.

This takes time to set up because you and your team members need to be documenting tasks and processes as they come up – so start early.

TIP:

Before you start the selling process, do a full audit of the team you have in place.

If you haven't extracted yourself from the business, you'll likely have to make a hire that takes over your duties – doing this before you exit raises the value and makes it 'turnkey' for a buyer.

This takes some time to identify and insert the right person – that's why planning your exit in advance is so crucial.

Start creating detailed SOPs (Standard Operating Procedures) of every process that your business does, big and small. This adds major value to the business.

Pull the Stats

As soon as your listing goes live, you'll be bombarded with requests for specific numbers from leads. Some of these will be 100% reasonable, others not so much.

We have a whole chapter coming up about your financials, but aside from your P&Ls themselves, there are key data pieces that buyers prioritize.

TIP:

Many important numbers will vary by industry, but some are evergreen, like:

- Gross income in the last 12 months (Trailing-12)
- Net income in the last 12 months (Trailing-12)
- Average profit margins
- Average cost to acquire a customer

- Breakdown of lead sources (ballparks are fine off the top of your head, but you should have a specific number for the Data Room)
- Average customer LTV
- Churn
- Customer concentration

*You should know these numbers enough that you can verbally answer when talking to buyers. The specific numbers should be in your Data Room that potential buyers get access to (after signing an NDA, of course).

Remember: Don't feel bad for not knowing every single number. Yes, you should be up to speed on the basics about your own business, but *not knowing every little thing can be a good sign* – it means you aren't in the weeds of the day-to-day or micromanaging. But you should at least be able to pull the information they need.

Audit your revenue sources and make sure you know what's most profitable. At this phase, you can consider making some tweaks to the business to double down on what's performing best. Many founders during this time actually realize that they can cut some offerings and tweak the business model to get their net profit up – which can add several figures to your sale price. The earlier you do this the better.

Now, at this point, you may need to put this book down and go implement what we've discussed so far. It might be a while before you return.

Many sellers spent months *or even a few years* in this phase we just covered, because setting up a business to be ready to sell can take a long time. It'll be worth it. This is where bringing in a consultant can make a huge difference.

Story Time: My First Experience with Brokers

Back when I owned my spa, I got a consultant one year before selling it. It's funny, I wasn't considering selling when I brought him on, but once we put all of the improvements in place, the profit grew so much that it was an easy target for buyers. I ended up getting a higher-than-average multiple, sold within 5 weeks flat.

I started it in 2012, and bootstrapped the heck out of it by pre-selling spa memberships to cover the buildout before even signing the lease. But the risk paid off: within 5 years we were the top-ranking location in San Diego.

I wasn't sold on the idea of using a broker, but advisors kept telling me that this one was too big to do alone. I had other thoughts: *Look, I've built this company from scratch. Why can't I use those same skills to list, market, and sell it?*

But to appease them I spoke with two brokers. I told them I wanted to go to market at a 4.5x multiple. I'll admit, that was high, but I knew I had something special. Even as an outsider in the industry, I was confident that there was so much more to a valuation than just the revenue and EBITDA (like the team, years in business, reputation, recurring revenue, etc).

This experience is burned into my brain because I want every business owner to get that target number. It *is* possible. With the clients I work with, I give them the option to go to market at that high number because there's a chance it sticks.

My favorite saying is: **"A company is worth what someone is willing to pay for it."**

So there I was running the 4.5x multiple by two brokers. Boy, did they try to make me feel like I was being outrageous and unrealistic.

One of them told me this:

> "It was good visiting with you today. I really like your business and feel that we could attract some serious buyers if we stay at/under that 3x multiple of your discretionary earnings. As I mentioned, only time will tell, but I'm not one to overprice a business just to get a listing and then try beating you down on price when we don't get any serious inquiries. I simply don't want

to waste my time or yours and, therefore, I think it's important to set realistic expectations and be completely honest with you. I want to get you the highest price possible as we both benefit from that."

The other broker said this:

"My guess would be between 2x adjusted cash flow plus present value of assets to 3x adjusted cash flow, including present value of assets."

I just wasn't willing to let it go for that. I knew it had more value.

Five short weeks later, I circled back to both of those brokers to let them know I'd sold for full price, all cash, at that 4.5x multiple. This is the value of taking the selling process into your own hands, or at least knowing how to differentiate a good broker.

Free resources from this chapter:

To access all the guides includes the Dream Buyer Exercise, Dream Sale Exercise, Questions to Ask a Broker, and more, you can *scan the code here:*

Before we go through every detail of the M&A process, here's a breakdown of what it looks like. There are granular parts to each stage, which we'll go over together in this book, but here's a birds-eye view.

M&A Process for Sellers (Self-Serve)

- Define your ideal sale (price, time frame, terms)
- Conduct a Gap Analysis to see how far you are from that outcome
- Implement the steps needed to get to that idea sale price
- Assemble your trusted advisors (CPA, lawyer, optional business intermediary)
- Optimize your team & hire new members to replace yourself as the owner
- Streamline your financials on an organized accounting software and categorize your inflow/outflow consistently
- Learn to pull your P&Ls and mark all add-backs to calculate your EBITDA/SDE (or with the help of your accountant)
- Create a custom NDA that potential buyers will have to sign before accessing the company name, Data Room, etc
- Create your Data Room where potential buyers will see all the business details
- Create the public listing for your business on all internet listing platforms
- Create a beautiful pitch deck to include in the Data Room,
- Respond to all incoming leads and get them on the phone before giving NDA then Data Room access
- Assertively follow up with all leads, moving them to LOI/IOI (written offer)
- Continue updating the Data Room with fresh data and business details addressing common questions/objections
- Negotiate LOIs and accept an LOI
- Enter into Due Diligence phase: create a Due Diligence folder with everything the buyer needs, set a closing date
- Work with the buyer, their lawyer, and your lawyer on the Purchase Agreement, then get it signed by both parties
- Keep growing and sprinting on your business all the way to the close date
- Hand off the company to the buyer

Chapter 3: Financials

"Ignoring financial tracking is like playing hide-and-seek with your money – spoiler alert: it always wins."

Ah, financials.

This process is serious, but it doesn't have to be painful.
I cannot stress to you how important your financials are – it's
the foundation of selling any business. It's one of the most
important, if not the most important thing to buyers.

Remember: one of the biggest points where deals fall apart is
during the DD (due diligence) phase because the financials
aren't matching up. This can be because the owner got lazy

when assembling the financials, missed something by accident, or misrepresented the numbers.

Think of it like doing your taxes: it's a lot of upfront work, and there's probably an accountant or CPA involved. But it's a lot worse if you do a messy job or leave it too late. You can do yourself a lot of favors by keeping clean records daily instead of having to problem-solve at the end.

You can either (A) do it thoroughly and do it right the first time, or (B) slack the first time and have to redo everything – which can cost you time, money, and a sale overall. I recommend the first one.

Depending on where your starting point is, here are some bare basics.

I've learned that nothing is common sense, so if you didn't know these, here you go. We'll build on this foundation.

> **TIP**:
> Before you start the process of selling your business, make sure you:
>
> - Are using an accounting software (like Quickbooks, Xero, etc.) for your business where all transactions are logged
> - Have designated business bank accounts
> - Separate your personal expenses
> - If you own other businesses, separate them completely
> - Combine everything into a single place – some founders start off as a different LLC or merge with another one which leaves you with multiple sets of P&Ls (not ideal)
>
> If you can't tick these boxes yet, start there.

If everything above is obvious to you, great. Let's move forward.

Before we dive into some key terms that buyers might bring up, I recommend that you don't tackle financials alone. A bookkeeper or accountant is 100% worth the money in the long run to get these dialed. Most business owners already use an accounting firm or bookkeeper on a monthly or quarterly basis.

Terms to Know

These are the common phrases you'll hear when selling your company, specifically related to numbers.

Acronym/Term	What It Means
P&L / PnL	Profit and Loss Statement This is a financial statement breaking down all income and expenses in a given time period (usually a longer period of time, like 12 months). It's one of the first things a buyer will look at to assess the company's profitability. You can export these statements from your accounting software. *Note: P&Ls should not be given to a buyer before an NDA has been signed. This information should be put in your Data Room for qualified buyers to see.
TTM / LTM / Trailing-12	Trailing 12 Months / Last 12 Months Buyers may ask for it in one of these acronyms, but it means the same thing. This is a type of P&L that covers (you guessed it) the last 12 full months up to the current month. That means if you are currently in September of 2023, the

	P&L would cover September 2022 through August 2023. *Note that it's easy to accidentally pull a start and end state of the same month (like August 2022 - August 2023), but this is 13 months, not 12.
Trailing-36	Trailing 36 Months / Last 36 Months This is the same type of statement to export as a TTM or Trailing-12, but it's of the past 36 months. This is a helpful way for buyers to see the company's trends over a long period of time.
Balance Sheet	This is a financial statement that provides a snapshot of the company's financial health at a specific point in time. It lists all the company's assets (what it owns), liabilities (what it owes), and equity. Unlike a Profit and Loss statement, which shows the business revenues and expenses over a period of time to show profitability, the balance sheet focuses on the company's current financial position at a given time.
Owner Operated	This means the owner is working in the business, not just on the business. They may be doing sales, amendment, fulfillment, or any other role that would have to be filled by someone new when

	the business is sold. When the current owner works in the business, sometimes their salary does not reflect an accurate market rate to perform those duties (it might be under market, meaning they are doing a lot of work and paying themselves less, or maybe they're taking a large salary for tasks/hours that a different hire could easily do. Calculate the reasonable cost to hire someone else to do all those owner's duties, and then you may have to add back some or subtract a more accurate one to get the proper final EBITDA/SDE.
EBITDA	Earnings Before Interest, Taxes, Depreciation, Amortization It's a term that helps buyers understand the overall financial performance of the company. This is a single number that can be shared publicly on your business listing. Formula: EBITDA = Net Income + Interest + Taxes + Depreciation + Amortization Generally this is used for mid to large-

	size businesses that are not owner-operated. The owner's salary is usually not included as an adjustment. Buyers may use it to calculate the value of a business by multiplying this number by the multiple they are using. Adjusted EBITDA: The same formula as above, but it adds or subtracts line items that are not part of the company's core operating performance. These can include one-time charges or credits, non-cash expenses, restructuring costs, or other irregularities that wouldn't transfer to the new owner. Its goal is to give an accurate snapshot of the earning potential if those irregularities were removed. *Be careful with these adjustments though: it's not uncommon for owners to get overly assertive with the add-backs to create a more profitable impression – you want to remain honest about the financial health of your company.
SDE	Seller's Discretionary Earnings Think of this like EBITDA, but for smaller businesses (typically businesses

	under \$1M) where the owner is involved and compensated. SDE takes into account the owner's pay as an adjustment. This is a single number that can be shared publicly on your business listing. Buyers may use it to calculate the value of a business by multiplying this number by the multiple they are using. The valuation multiple used for SDE is often smaller than an EBITDA multiple because of owner involvement. Of course, this depends on countless other factors including the unique business, industry, etc. – but assuming two companies are the same, just know that it's safe to assume an owner-operated business using SDE will have a smaller multiple than an EBITDA counterpart.
Add-back	These are non-operating expenses that get added back to the net profit in the P&L because they would not be costs for the new owner to do business. They are more common with an owner-operated business calculating SDE, because you may have written off semi-personal expenses under the business that the new owner will not need to

pay.

Common examples of add-backs include:

- Your personal car lease & discretionary transportation that was charged to the company
- Interest on business loans or credit card fees
- Legal and business intermediary fees related to selling the business
- "Gray area" add-backs are one-time expenses that are not necessarily completely personal, but the new owner would not have to pay for them. Breaking them out can help the buyer understand a more accurate profit they would make as a new owner without those nonessential expenses. These include things like website redesigns, attending conferences, expensive masterminds, consultants, and coaches. Another unexpected potential add-back is the salary costs of excess previous employees if you were

	overstaffed and have since let them go (the SBA allows this one). A good way to approach these "gray area" addbacks is to highlight them in a separate color on your P&Ls so a buyer can easily distinguish them. *At the end of this chapter you can **scan the code** for a full downloadable list of common potential add-backs that we share with clients
Turnkey	Think of this as the *opposite* of owner-operated: a business is turnkey if a new owner could take over and everything would run as normal. Usually it means team members and systems are in place so the new owner does not have to step in and run it hands-on at all.
Owners Draws / Distributions / Personal Draws	These are funds deducted from the company accounts that show up on the financials, separate from an involved owner's normal salary or pay. For example, as the owner, you might need an extra $2k to cover expenses, so you pull it as an Owner's Draw or a Distribution. Alternatively, some owners opt not to take a salary and

<table>
<tr><td></td><td>instead draw funds from the company accounts when needed. These transactions will be reflected on the balance sheet rather than the P&L. If the owner is on a salary, it will be shown on the P&L.</td></tr>
</table>

Let's practice. You can always flip back here if you get an email like this (happens all the time). They message you:

"Hi. Pls share LTM (last twelve months) and most current balance sheet. Thx."

→ How do you respond to this?

You should never give your financials out freely, without speaking to them first on the phone. Make sure they have access to capital first and are a serious buyer.

After you've qualified them, you can provide standard reports like the TTM and balance sheet. You don't need to pull these reports each time someone asks for them – you need only do it once and put it in the data room. The buyer will see them in there when you grant them access to that whole area (don't worry, there's a full section on how to set up your data room in the next chapter). Ask yourself:

1. First of all, if the person sending that message has already signed your NDA, they should have seen those reports in the data room so you can resend them the link to that folder and remind them that it's all inside.
2. If they have not signed the NDA and are just messaging you this, hoping they can get this info anyway (the likely scenario), here's all you have to say:

Hey _____, these full financials are in the data room, happy to give you access once the NDA is signed. (hyperlink the NDA in the email for them).

This protects you from potential competitors, or even other people selling their companies that want comps on your business without signing anything first. For a genuine interested buyer, these aren't an issue. Some of them might try to make you think it's standard practice to share a full P&L with them before signing an NDA, but in our experience, don't do it.

TIP:

Not sure what your P&L should look like?

We have three examples for you in our free bonuses section (scan the code here to get them):

It includes a:

- Digital PR firm P&L
- Subscription box company P&L
- CRM customization agency P&L

*These three capture a mix of service and product businesses, including physical and digital, some with office space and some without, so you can see the differences in line items. The nuances will vary by industry, but this can help get you on the right track. A good intermediary should assist you with P&Ls, like we do with our clients, but you can also do them completely on your own.

Here's a visual reference (real ones are in the link above):

Profit and Loss
November 2020 - October 2021

	Nov 2020	Dec 2020	Jan 2021	Feb 2021	Mar 2021	Apr 2021	May 2021	Jun 2021	Jul 2021	Aug 2021	Sep 2021	Oct 2021	Total

Income													
Advertising Income													
Commission Income													
Loan Discount/Credit/ProSome													
Marketing Income													
Uncategorized Income													
Total Income													
Cost of Goods Sold													
Total Cost of Goods Sold													
Gross Profit													
Expenses													
Total Expenses													
Net Operating Income													
Net Income													

How Often to Update Financials While on the Market

The most transparent approach is to export new P&Ls for every new completed month prior and plug them into the data room. This means your TTM will change each month, and your EBITDA/SDE may shift slightly too.

→ *Do I need to update the numbers on all the listings every month as my SDE changes?*

If it's a significant or unexpected change, yes. For example, if you lost clients or had a massive dip in business and this won't necessarily correct itself next month, you should update the net and gross numbers on your public listing to stay transparent about what a buyer can expect. Nothing turns them off of a business faster than discovering that the financials have been misrepresented with higher numbers.

*In fact, you want the opposite effect: your business should be increasing in revenue month-over-month as you have it listed – this is what gets buyers interested in making the purchase and puts you in the drivers' seat to receive competing bids.

Next, we move onto the exciting part: bringing your business to the public market.

Chapter 4:
Listing for Sale

"What's your business worth? It's worth exactly what someone is willing to pay for it."

First of all, *great job* – you've done the hard work preparing your business to sell. That's one of the toughest and longest stages, but you made it through. Now it's time to get the amazing company you've built in front of buyers.

Your business listing package is one of the most important things you'll ever put together.

Think of it this way: every piece of information that you have here is going to *attract* or *repel* specific buyers. This is why we take this process *very seriously* – it requires the right strategy behind the scenes before the business goes live.

You May Be Able to Sell *Without* Listing Your Company for Sale

First of all, let's save you some work by seeing if we can skip you to the finish line. Before you do all the work of listing the business, you might be able to find a buyer *without* even having to post it anywhere. It's actually common.

Think of it like buying or selling a house off-market: a lot of the best transactions are private party deals. They stay under the radar by leveraging relationships and connections to bypass entire phases (and the costs that come with them).

That's why I recommend working through off-market opportunities before you go to the open internet. This can include:

- Create a database of similar business owners and use software like Snov.io to scrape their emails and reach out personally
- Find ideal acquirers on LinkedIn and contact them there
- Pitch your business in off-market deal communities (we have one called the Rapid Acquisition Club™ that's been successful for sellers)
- Leverage your personal network to see who knows who

- Speak with competitors but use these exact words: *"If I ever planned on selling in the future, would you have any interest, that way I can go to you first?"*
- Talk to your employees to see if one (or several) of them wants to take over the business

---

TIP:

Before listing your business for sale on all the platforms, **go in-house first to your team. One of them may want to purchase the company.** Employee buyouts are generally smooth.

If you have any great employees that would be a fit to take over the business, talk to them individually to see if any of them would want to buy it.

Don't just pull them aside and say you're thinking of selling; instead, say you're thinking of bringing in an investor or partner, but since they understand the business so well and are already deeply involved in it, you wanted to give them the opportunity and would they be interested?

*An employee buying your company may be less experienced or familiar with the buying process or have less access to capital, but that's ok. If they can qualify for an SBA loan and the company is in good hands, it's still worth exploring.

NDAs

As soon as you get potential buyers on the phone, they need to sign a simple NDA (Non-Disclosure Agreement) before you tell them the business name or let them into the Data Room.

There are lots of NDAs on the internet, and we are *not* lawyers, so don't swap this out for legal advice. We'd get in trouble for giving you legal templates here, so choose the one that's best for you.

TIP:

One important thing to note here: it's important to customize the NDA to your business *without* putting the business name on the NDA itself (otherwise you've doxed your company before they've signed it). An easy way to personalize an otherwise 'templated' NDA is to title it the specific type of business yours is and add this in the first paragraph tool.

> → *Example:* Let's say you own a digital marketing agency. In the first paragraph, instead of saying something like "in regard to the business", consider making it say "in regard to the digital marketing agency", etc. This gives specificity. You get the point.

Prep the Data Room

Your Data Room needs to be ready **before** you list your business because it's the first place that you'll send vetted leads. Not only is it the most important thing to them, it's also the biggest phase that prospective buyers give you a *Yes* or *No*.

You want your Data Room to be detailed enough that it answers all their questions and gives them a complete picture of the business – enough to make an offer. You don't want to accidentally include things in the Data Room that should be left for later in the Due Diligence process, this can put your business at a disadvantage by revealing too much. For example, customer info (without names!) is fine at this stage (stats on what % of leads are from each lead source, stats on the average order value, cost to acquire, average demographics of clients, etc). All that is fine. But *do not* mention your specific vendors by name or your customer names at this stage.

We always create extensive Data Rooms for our clients, and you should try to do the same.

Why are good Data Rooms so valuable?

First, they allow the buyer to write a more confident offer. Detailed, organized information gives them a deep understanding of your company upfront, which means they're making an informed decision instead of a blind offer that's less likely to be serious.

Second, a well-made Data Room will save so much time during Due Diligence because you provided a lot of the necessary resources upfront. We will cover Due Diligence in detail in chapter 7.

Here's what should be in your Main Data Room:
- P&Ls from your past 3 years (with add-backs), plus TTM (flip back a few pages if you need a refresher of what these are)
- FAQs about the business (you can add to this as questions from buyers come in)
- List of your Owners Duties
- Org Chart (if you have one)
- Stats/data that pertain to your unique business (site traffic, backlinks, general customer stats)
- A pitch deck if you're fancy
- A CIM (Confidential Information Memorandum – (optional) this is a hefty document that breaks down the business in detail. It's common for larger companies and is pretty time-consuming to put together
- Relevant press and media visibility

What to Include in the Public Listing
Now you're at the phase where it's time to create the listing.

Take this seriously: this is "first impressions" at its peak. The listing is what gets leads into your inbox, submitting their information. Something has to convert them to take action.

Of course, a lot of this will come down to the facts of your business and how strong it is. But marketing and framing is 100% real here too. I've helped sellers who were listed for months with little to no bites, then we came in and changed the copy of the listing, along with the image, and within a week had great buyer leads.

Here's what makes a great for-sale listing:

Listing Platforms
Of course, one of the most important factors is where you list your business. There are endless listing sites, but only a handful are heavy hitters. Here's an overview of the most popular ones and things to keep in mind for each.

Platform	What to Know	Fees (as of late 2023)
BizBuySell	Most of our buyers come from BBS. It's a great classic. If you only had to list in one place it'd be this. *Yes it's a slightly dated platform, but your success selling on here depends on the quality of your listing. All types of businesses get listed here at all sizes. You can set yourself apart on here with great copywriting and plenty of details in your listing – there are so many bad/incomplete listings on here. We also like that leads get sent directly to your email instead of messaging directly on the platform.	Flat rate *(great perk) - no % taken of sale price!* We love that BBS keeps it real with a flat rate to list instead of taking a % of the sale price. It also has the largest exposure and traffic. For a 6-month term, Basic listings are $65.95/month, Showcase listings are $89.95/month, and Diamond Listings are $199.95/month. The higher the listing level, the more exposure to buyers.

MicroAcquire (now called Acquire)	Buyers and sellers on here tend to be younger in our experience. *This is a newer platform so the user experience is more all-inclusive, if you prefer that. It's especially good for digital businesses, SaaS, and startups. Keep in mind that they have all the messaging directly on the platform as well as the business detail sharing – their goal is for you to communicate with the buyer fully on there. They even have an option to make and accept offers directly on the platform. Personally, we like the ability to move buyers off the platform so we can personalize our	4% of sale price

	own flow of communication to Data Room and offers, but others like it all on the site.	
Flippa	This one is specifically for online/digital businesses. It's also self-serve, so instead of emailing with leads, it's also done on the platform. Offers can be made within too.	Sliding scale % of sale price (depending on size), PLUS a listing fee. Ranges between 5% to 10% depending on sale price. Also, to create a listing, the listing fee ranges from $49 to $599.
Empire Flippers	This is also for online/digital businesses. It's also self-serve, so instead of emailing with leads, it's also done on the platform. Offers can be made within too.	Sliding scale % of sale price (depending on size). The commission structure is blended, so the commission rates are stacked based on the value of the business.Here's how it breaks down: • Under $700,000 –

		Commission is a flat 15% on the sale price. • For a business between $700,000 and $5M – Commission is 8% on the amount above $700,000 and below $5M. • For a business above $5 million – Commission is to 2.5% on the amount above $5M.
Dealstream	All types of businesses can be listed and sold on here. Leads come in via email (not messaging within the platform).	Monthly flat rate subscription- *no % taken of sale price!* They have a *free* basic listing option of a $45/mo subscription which gives you additional visibility.

*Note: Fees may change on each platform, these are the most current ones we have access to, as of writing this in 2023.

Copywriting

The written description of your listing is a huge factor. You are trying to attract the right acquirer while repelling the wrong ones. You also have a limited number of characters per platform to sum up the entire business, its major selling points, and trajectory. It's super important to be detailed here, but also remember that readability matters. The goal is to get an inquiry and conversation going, so you can follow up with details as needed. Some listings are these huge walls of paragraphs which drastically reduces how much people will actually read it. Try to remove fluffy adjectives and offer bullet points where possible, while still highlighting the advantages of the business.

Here's a few phrases buyers love to see (*if* applicable to your business). I call them the "favorite R-words":

- *Relocatable/Remote:* Digital businesses that can be operated remotely are especially valuable and often easier to scale. They are also accessible to a wider pool of buyers who can run it hands-off.
- *Recurring Revenue:* These business models are especially appealing – they provide consistent

cash to the business with a calculable ROI which can present it as a safer investment.

- *Retention:* Speaking of recurring revenue, bonus points if the business has high customer retention. This means clients are sticking around for a long time without churning out.
- *Removal of Owner:* A company can command a higher sale price when they have successfully removed the owner (you) as a dependency in the business – that means the founder is unraveled from sales, fulfillment, and ideally from the brand and front of house.

Photos

Most listing platforms give you an option to upload a photo with the listing. If it's a platform that offers this, always add one. This makes the listing stand out above the lazy ones that have no images.

*But this is **important**:* Use a stock photo / public creative commons image / AI generated image that accurately captures your business, not a literal personal photo you have. People could reverse- image search it to figure out the company, so it's safest to do this to remove those risks.

Details

The more detail the better. Even if a field is not required, it's best to fill it out. Some people avoid putting the gross revenue and/or cash flow on the listing, and just put an asking price. We don't recommend this – most buyers will perceive this as a business in unhealthy standing. In a buyer's head they're thinking: *if the business had a healthy EBITDA, there's no reason they'd exclude it.*

It's your job to break down all the assets of your company. This is what differentiates it from competitors or startups and makes it worth buying. Sometimes these assets are things you don't realize are incredibly valuable, but it is to a buyer. They can include:

- Team
- Systems
- Years in business (the longer the better)
- Market share
- Email database
- Client list, especially if they are big names
- Trademarks and IP
- Domains
- Social media following
- Brand recognition, reputation, and online presence (including online reviews/ratings, media features)

- Stats: Lower churn rate than industry average, etc.

Go Live

At this point you're ready to list your business and hit "Publish". If you're posting on several listing platforms, which I suggest you do, try to go live all on the same day so you can consistently track how long it's been on the market.

TIP:

Is there an optimal day to list your business?

This is a common question.
First off, let me stress that a well-written, detailed listing is the thing that brings in leads – *not* the time you post the ad.

That being said, there are some things that give you a little boost.

We find that early on Fridays is a good time to list because it's less likely to get lost in the sea, and many good buyers are on the hunt during the weekend so they can find it more easily this way.

This is just an anecdote though, never rush your listing to fit into a time frame. Focus on making it accurate and compelling to the point that your perfect buyer wouldn't be able to leave the page without inquiring.

Updating the Listing Details

There are plenty of cases where you may need to make some tweaks to increase your chances of success. As soon as the listing goes live, keep note of the inquiries and listing stats (if the platform offers it).

For example, BizBuySell shows you stats of weekly impressions and leads, which you can use to gameplan tweaks if needed.

- If you're getting a lot of views/impressions but very low inquiries, we can guess that the title and image are solid enough to get them to click, but the actual listing details aren't converting them so that's what needs work.
- If you're getting very low clicks/impressions, it's the initial listing information that isn't enticing people enough. Consider updating the image, headline, or category.

Another area to continue updating is when you start talking to leads: if you are consistently getting specific areas of confusion, consider updating the listing to clarify. The goal is to speak their language.

Updating the Data Room

Best-case scenario is that you get bites immediately on your business.

But if it sits for some time on the market, the Data Room may become outdated. Let's say you listed your business in July, but now it's September. All the financials in the Data Room will be through June. Your public listing will also have a Gross Revenue and SDE/EBITDA as of June. Even if the company numbers have been stable (or ideally grown), at this point it's a good move to update everything with the most current numbers.

Chapter 5:
Leads & Inquiries

"The fortune is in the follow-up." – Jim Rohn

The 4 Buyer Types: Know Who You're Dealing With
To succeed in selling your business, you need to know your counterpart inside out. Understanding buyer types is key for determining your company's value and crafting an effective negotiation strategy with each person.

You'll encounter so many different buyers in the lead process, but most of the time, they'll fall into one of these:

1. *Individual Buyer:*
   Individual buyers are motivated by income and

freedom. They seek low-risk investments and prefer businesses with proven track records. To attract individual buyers, focus on minimizing perceived risks and avoid overwhelming them with information.

2. *Financial Buyer:*
   Financial buyers, like private equity groups, are solely driven by numbers and ROI (Return on Investment). They aim to generate high returns and often retain the existing management team. To appeal to financial buyers, concentrate on building a strong management team and increasing EBITDA.

3. *Strategic Buyer:*
   Strategic buyers are ideal purchasers and typically pay a premium for your business. Their goal is to increase market share, aiming to take over your established customer relationships to expedite lengthy sales cycles and potentially cross-sell to them.

   In times of low unemployment when hiring top talent is tricky, and a company is scaling rapidly, an *"Acquihire"* might be one of their main reasons behind purchasing your company.

   Ac·qui·hire: an act or instance of buying out a company primarily for the skills and expertise of its staff, rather than for the products or services it supplies.

Strategic buyers are focused on long-term integration and synergy. To attract them, emphasize the unique value your business can immediately bring to their firm. These are great buyers to consider for a private acquisition where you engage with them before listing publicly. If it works out, you don't even have to go through the time-consuming go-to-market phase.

4. *Industry Buyer:*
    Industry buyers are often the last resort and typically pay lower prices. They won't pay for goodwill and they only value what can't be easily replicated. Selling to industry buyers requires especially careful negotiation, protection of confidential information, and building unique value.

Mergers, Acquisitions, Roll-ups, Bolt-ons

Depending on the type of buyer, they will have different goals and plans for your business when they take over.

While some of these terms like roll-up and tuck-in sound exciting, be wary of a first-time roll-up. If the buyer hasn't done it before, the integration is *hard*. Someone I know wanted to do a roll up of 10 landscaping companies, and he was having an insanely hard time trying to integrate just the first two. Imagine doing that 8 more times?

If you go with this type of buyer, you have to consider everything that needs to be merged or changed, because it will be rolled into their current company processes. This includes the team, software systems, HR, employee healthcare coverage, payroll company, client pricing, branding, and so much more.

I've personally done a few rollups with my cleaning company and my wellness spa. Although they were small ones, they still came with complexities that I never even thought of until the deal was already done. A big one is pricing. A smart acquirer could acquire a company that charges much less than their current company, sometimes half, and once they take over, continue honoring that price for clients to keep them. It would be wise to pay team members their normal commission on that service provided. Seems like a loss leader upfront, but it pays off and the acquirer profits at the end of the day at scale. Always look at the big picture, especially with the other advantages of grabbing market share.

I had a friend who had his large printing company listed for sale and came across an opportunity to pick up another one at a steal. This would have bumped up the overall multiple on his exit price based on how significantly the EBITDA would increase. He sold his company before he committed to this acquisition, but this could have been a major

This may not come up for you, but it's something to keep in mind if the opportunity comes your way. The buyer will probably have you stay on a bit if the integration is not fully complete, which is understandable, so use this to filter which is the right fit for you.

Questions You Need to Ask

Here's some key questions to make sure the person you're talking to is actually a potential fit to buy your business – the goal is to identify as quickly as possible whether or not this is a waste of anyone's time.

Ask questions like:
- What specific types of businesses have you been in the market for?
- What attracted you to this business?
- Have you bought a business before? Have you owned a business before?
- How long have you been looking? How seriously have you been shopping?
- What is your experience in this industry?
- Do you have access to capital? How much?

How to Vet & Qualify Leads

Now that you have an overview of the types of buyers you'll

encounter, let's walk through the right 'flow' to follow once a lead comes in.

Every sale comes down to the interaction.

Again, the goal when you chat with each lead is to get them off email and onto a real phone call, or ideally a Zoom so you can pull more cues from their expression, enthusiasm, body language, etc.

Here's the correct order of interacting with buyer leads:
1. Inquiry comes in: respond to their message and try to get them on the phone ASAP
2. If they listed their phone number, immediately give them a call (a 5-minute chat is plenty). It's important to get them on the phone to initially qualify.
    - *Sometimes with a strong buyer, this first conversation goes so well that you end the call verbally agreeing to give them Data Room access. If this happens, send them the NDA link while on the phone and get them to sign it right then, so you can let them in the Data Room as soon as you hang up.
3. Leads who have been vetted with a personal conversation (at least a phone call where you get a feel for their experience, enough to stalk them on LinkedIn

as well as gauge how serious they are) can be granted access to the Data Room

4. Follow-up questions will come from them as they dive deeper into your business and the Data Room, once you've given access. This is a good sign – it means their moving towards an offer. Depending on the depth of these, jump back on a call to go into detail. Zoom is great, but in-person is the gold standard if possible.

How to Follow Up

Follow-up is hands-down one of the most important things to do – and it's a *lot* to manage.

This is one of the biggest reasons that business owners use us: the amount of time and energy it takes just to follow up with every lead and manage each relationship is a full-time job – not to mention that at the same time you're running and growing a business that needs to be showing healthy and ideally, growing revenues.

Our clients even have our main phone number they can call or text anytime that routes to all team members, including my personal cell number.

One of my favorite mantras:
"Deals don't sleep."

→ A great intermediary should be ready to take calls

and meetings at any time, including the middle of the night (we have international clients), as well as during Thanksgiving, Christmas, etc. The fourth quarter is usually the busiest time of the year – large companies are aiming to unload cash from their balance sheets before the end of the year for tax reasons. So they look to acquire other companies which helps secure market share for a strong start to the upcoming year.

However, our success fee reflects that level of service we provide. I'm not shy about telling prospective clients that we are usually more expensive than most other M&A advisors, but we easily justify it by getting sellers far more than they wanted, so it covers our fees.

If you want to run your business while managing the leads, you *can* do it yourself. Just keep in mind that the most important job you have at the end of the day is keeping the business healthy: the numbers should be increasing month-over-month while it's listed and through offers to have real negotiating leverage. Don't lag on running the business for the sake of focusing on the selling process. If you keep the company thriving it will sell itself more easily.

For those of you going the self-managed route and talking to leads yourself, we have a **super simple spreadsheet template** you can download at the end of this chapter to track all of your potential buyer inquiries. We love our CRM but understand that not all sellers have access to one. If you already have a CRM system in your company, you can definitely use that as well.

Gatekeeping – How Much is Too Much?

Listen, vetting leads is important. It's a 2-way interview.

But some brokers are so unfriendly and exclusionary to leads that it can rule out buyers that might have been suitable. They make a lot of assumptions about who "isn't a fit" instead of just finding out.

Your goal shouldn't be to disqualify them, it's to give them information and let them disqualify themselves.

> → *Example:*
> A lot of buyers right now are first-timers who are testing out the 'search process' and have idyllic dreams of buying a business with "no money down". It doesn't help that entrepreneurship influencers are popularizing this concept, which is great that acquisitions are becoming mainstream – but it brings with it some unsophisticated buyers which are easy to identify.
>
> If you aren't comfortable with seller financing (carrying some of the purchase price for the buyer as a loan), this matters. This can come up in the first or

second conversation with a potential buyer. Say something like: "the right buyer for this business has access to capital in the full amount of the purchase price. Seller carry isn't something we're open to, so if that's the type of acquisition you're looking for it might be best to look at other options where the demand isn't as competitive." Doesn't have to be verbatim. But the nice thing about saying this is that it gets across the point that high-quality businesses that are in-demand get cash buyers. Struggling businesses or situations with an urgent need to sell might allow that, but you aren't in a position of scarcity.

Asking Buyers to Show ID or Proof of Funds?

There is a point where *you have to balance the desire for security with the importance of removing friction.*

I've seen listings where the seller/broker immediately asks for a copy of the interested buyer's driver's license *and/or* proof of funds from the bank, their current credit score, how much their home is worth *just* to get into the Data Room. That's overkill.

Honestly, a lot of brokers do this because they're lazy and it makes their job easier. The more hoops they can make the other person jump through, the less work for them.

The goal is to make it a seamless experience for prospective buyers that still respects your company's privacy. You want to drip out the right amount of information at the right time. We think a signed NDA, *as well as a* personal phone conversation (**both of these**, not one or the other) is enough to give Data Room access. You can always remove access if they go unresponsive (this is where it helps to have a specific data room software at scale like we do, or you just have to do a lot of manual management).

Also – if you're doing a DIY Data Room setup in Google Drive or somewhere similar, make sure that you personalize the settings of each document in the data room to be private and non-downloadable. A lot of people do this in Google Drive – the problem there is that the buyer leads can see who else the folder and inner documents are shared with, which isn't great. A lot of listing sites have places where you can upload data room-type documents to automate this. In our experience, they don't have the personalization that we prefer.

Selling to a Competitor: Pros & Cons
It's very common that competitors will be interested in acquiring your business – but *be very careful.*
It's an easy recipe for getting taken advantage of.

→ An **asshole competitor** will express initial interest in acquiring your business, just to get into the data room to see information like your P&Ls, customer demographics, customer LTV, how you structure your offers, your lead sources, industry-specific information, etc. and then say it's not the right fit (newsflash: they were never planning on buying it, they just wanted intel on the inner workings of your company).

→ A *super* **asshole competitor** will do all the things above and get into the data room, but they won't stop there – they'll actually submit an offer / LOI. This does 2 things:
1. It makes them look legit serious about buying the company, so you don't suspect anything
2. If you accept the offer, it goes to Due Diligence before close – in this phase, *even more information* about your company becomes available for them to see. Then they pull out before closing saying that something they uncovered during this phase didn't look right. Or they'll make up some BS excuse about funding falling through / not seeing the ROI of the acquisition anymore, etc. You get the picture.

Here are some ways to protect yourself from getting played:
- Have them sign a custom NDA – one that's well-drafted in your favor – before they get access to the Data Room. We do this for all our clients. Do not

share the P&Ls / other business information before they've signed it. If they don't want to, there's a reason.
- If you do get to the offer phase and they do seem genuinely interested in making an offer, take a non-refundable deposit if they back out. This will help weed out some shady behavior.

Remember that these two precautions don't protect you from anything – bad actors can find workarounds, but deterrents help.

When a competitor acquires your business, the value of your company lies in different things than in a normal acquisition – it's now the customers that are adding the most value.

All the scary parts aside, competitors can sometimes be the ideal buyers. We've seen and worked with them before. It can be a perfect strategic move for them to vertically acquire your business and fold it into theirs, taking market share while shrinking competition. They already have the fulfillment systems and industry knowledge to succeed.

Free resources from this chapter:

To access all the guides includes the Lead Tracking template from this chapter, P&L templates, and more, you can *scan the code here:*

Chapter 6:
The Art of LOIs: Maneuvering Letters of Intent Like a Pro

"Having multiple offers on the table is not like comparing apples to apples. It's more like comparing apples to carrots to candy bars." - Christine McDannell

---

So, you're at the LOI: the Letter of Intent stage. This is where things get real. It's like a serious conversation about commitment in a relationship. It's not the wedding, but it's not just talking anymore. You're laying the engagement out.

It's one thing to have people interested in buying your business; it's a whole other skill to get them to commit and put their money where their mouth is.

Selling your business is a little like a poker game: you've shown your cards up to a point, and now it's time for the prospective buyer to meet you there. This is where the Letter of Intent (LOI) comes into play—a pivotal document that sets the course for your exit journey.

This chapter will guide you through the intricacies of Letters of Intent, from getting buyers to submit them, to understanding the various types of financing options, and of course the ground rules for what's reasonable.

This is the nitty-gritty that separates the 'never-been-sold' from successful dealmakers.

> **What is an LOI?**
>
> Simply put, an LOI is a written offer.
>
> It's not legally binding, except for a few parts like confidentiality. Both the buyer and seller sign it.
>
> This agreement outlines the deal's basic terms and conditions, like price and structure. It sets the stage to move toward the Due Diligence and final negotiation to the Purchase Agreement.

Terms to Know

These are the common phrases you'll hear during the offer stages of selling a business.

Acronym/Term	What It Means
LOI	*Letter of Intent* An LOI declares a buyer's intent to purchase the business and outlines the preliminary terms of the sale. It usually includes essential elements like purchase price, deal structure, timelines, confidentiality, and

	sometimes an exclusivity agreement. It's your job to discuss each of these points with a potential buyer, ideally before the LOI is submitted, but also after it's submitted so you can move to common ground and sign it to lock things in further. Think of it like asking for marriage: it doesn't transfer ownership or lock thighs down completely; it just communicates *intent* to buy the business. As a seller, once you accept an LOI, you move to the next stage.
IOI	*Indication of Interest* This is very similar to an LOI: it communicates intent to purchase. The difference with this term vs. LOI is that an IOI is often used for larger acquisitions, $10M and higher, so it's the first non-binding stage of expressing written interest. Just like an LOI, an IOI will include the offered price range and deal structure.
DD	*Due Diligence* This is the phase you enter once an offer has been accepted in writing and

	you are moving toward the finish line. The goal here is for the buyer to get access to all necessary business details (this often includes internal processes as well as financial data like tax returns to verify the business materials before signing the Purchase Agreement.
PA / APA	*Purchase Agreement / Asset Purchase Agreement* This is the legal contract that comes after an LOI is accepted and after basic Due Diligence is done. In the Purchase Agreement, the terms and conditions of the sale and purchase of assets or shares of a company are broken down in detail.
MOU	*Memorandum of Understanding* The Memorandum of Understanding (MOU) is a non-legally binding agreement between two or more parties outlining the terms and details, including each parties' requirements and responsibilities. For larger deals, this comes after an IOI and is one layer deeper in the process.
Closing	Closing refers to the finalization of a

	transaction, where all relevant documents are signed, and funds are transferred, concluding the transaction, and resulting in the transfer of ownership of the asset or company. After closing, you are officially no longer the owner.
Seller Carry / Seller's Note	This is a method of financing where the seller acts as a lender to the buyer. Basically you are acting like the bank, letting the buyer pay a portion of the purchase price back to you over time with interest. This is often used to bridge a financing gap in the sale of a business, when there is still a portion of the price owed and the loan or buyer's personal funds do not cover it, but you want the deal to work. We don't recommend carrying any more than 20% of the sale price this way – our logic is, if the buyer needs more than that financed by the seller, then the business is probably out of their price range. You will charge interest on this loan (often ranging from 6-12% interest). A good rule of thumb is to match the current rate that the SBA is charging. The shorter the seller carry term, the

	better. Two years is a comfortable term but you may need to go up to five years depending on the amount. However, if there is an SBA loan involved, the seller carry cannot be "senior debt" to the SBA loan, so usually that means it has to be over the same duration as the SBA loan.
Earnout	This is a contractual provision stating that the seller of a business will receive additional payments based on the future performance of the business once the buyer takes over. This is often used to close a valuation gap between a buyer and a seller. Buyers try to add them more often because it creates a feeling of risk reduction since the payment is based on how much the business is making in the new owner's hands. I personally try to avoid Earnouts, especially if they are requesting you to stay with the company full time until you achieve it. Earnouts can be an effective way to justify a higher purchase price for your business, especially if you're comfortable with taking the risk of betting on the company's

<table>
<tr><td></td><td>performance in their hands instead of a clear-cut guaranteed amount you'll receive. Try not to do more than 20% of the sale price as an earnout.</td></tr>
</table>

Getting the Buyer to Submit an LOI

Usually it takes some coaxing to get a buyer to write the LOI – even if they're serious and seem like a good fit. If you're just answering buyers' questions but not raising the conversation of an offer, it's far less likely they'll just land in your lap. You need to guide them there.

If a buyer is serious about acquiring your business, they need to prove it by submitting an LOI. So, how do you nudge them into action?

Be Transparent but Time-sensitive:
Time kills all deals. It's important to convey the right sense of urgency to prospective buyers– one that urges them to act but doesn't scare them off or seem fake. Let them know other parties are interested (if that's the case- never lie) and set an offer date that you will review all LOIs. Humans respond to deadlines.

Use a 3rd Party Advantage:
If you are using someone to assist you with the sale and

negotiations, like a broker, they really come in handy here. There's something about a 3rd party speaking on behalf of the seller that really makes a big difference. It's an emotional transaction and that can cloud your judgment. Maybe you really love the potential buyer, so you quickly drop the price for them?

Be Friendly & Firm

You want to deliver structured demands in a digestible way. A lot of times, potential buyers will say something like, "Oh, we're a little too close to your Offer Date, so we're going to pass." To this, you *always* want to try to get an offer out of them. The goal of the deadline is to get offers, not drive them away. You can respond to this by softening the perceived commitment. Let them know it's just a first stage of throwing their hat in the ring and it's non-binding. They might also say something like "I don't feel comfortable submitting an offer right now because the price we have in mind is pretty far from what you want and we don't want to offend you" or something like that. When this happens, just tell them that's fine, *just to submit something in writing*, whatever their current offer is. You can go from there.

Remove the Burden

The less they feel like they have to do, the better. One of the best ways to reduce friction is to provide potential buyers with an LOI template. It's a real undertaking for them to loop in lawyers to draft an LOI, so sharing with them a simple template can shortcut the process and reduce the perceived burden. It also will be templated with the basic protections that you want, which reduces the amount of negotiating that you have to do if they write their own from scratch.

An Offer Came in – Now What?

First of all, congratulations.

Now we want to assess the LOI (or hopefully multiple LOIs) that you have on the table.

TIP:

Remember, **the highest price offer isn't necessarily the best one.**

Here's where you dance between valuation and terms. It's not always about the highest price; it's about the best deal with the *highest likelihood to close.*

If someone is offering more but they don't have much cash in the bank, you need to consider: How likely is it for this loan to clear at this price? How will they come up with the funds otherwise?

> Know your trade-offs. Understand the structure, because the last thing you want is to get played in your own game.

Exclusivity

Be Careful with Overarching Requests

When the talk turns to exclusivity, tread carefully. It signals that things are serious, but it also ties your hands. Don't let the buyer take you off the market for too long without a firm commitment.

I have **two major tips** for you here:

1. If the buyer is firm on exclusivity, have them agree on modified language that still allows you to keep the listing live on all the listing platforms, with a line added to the top if the description saying "LOI Accepted" or "Currently Under Offer, Accepting Backups" (if the buyer allows). It's a huge disadvantage for you to pull the listings down completely.
2. On top of this, a buyer might insert exclusivity language into the LOI that you cannot speak with or respond to any inquiries if their offer is accepted. This is common, but it's wise for you

to rework the language so the buyer understands that you will still receive leads because the listing will stay up, and that you will respond to each lead letting them know that it is currently under offer with exclusivity, but you will let them know if anything changes. This way you continue to collect the contact information of those leads, which is important for you to have in your reserves.

Keep Playing the Field

Until any exclusivity clause hits (after you sign the LOI), you're not tied down. Keep the conversation going with other interested parties. It keeps the pressure on the potential buyer and can serve as a backup if things go south. Even better if the buyer didn't include one in the LOI, so you are free to keep collecting backup leads.

Deposits & Earnest Money

Earnest money is the buyer's way of saying, "Hey, I'm serious about this." They put down a deposit, akin to a pledge, which is then securely held in an escrow account. This cash is managed by a third-party escrow service or can be held in your lawyer's trust account, potentially saving both the buyer and seller on escrow fees (typically split between both parties).

Importantly, this deposit will be credited towards the final price when the deal is completed.

Think of escrow as your impartial outsider holding onto cash or assets while you and the buyer hash things out. They hold onto the buyer's deposit and won't release it until everything is confirmed by both sides and it's time to close.

When you're negotiating the sale of your business, you might ask for a deposit from the buyer – usually $10,000 - $20,000, which they'll put in an escrow account. That money stays put during the whole due diligence.

Escrow holds the funds, making sure both sides keep their end of the deal. This way, if the buyer backs out, you aren't left empty-handed (assuming the reason for the buyer backing out was no fault of your own). Make sure the language is crystal-clear, specifying that this will be considered a "Breakup Fee" if they change their mind.

On the other hand, if the deal falls through because their funding (like an SBA loan) fell through, they are entitled to receive the full deposit back. Make this distinction in the contract.

It shouldn't be an issue for a buyer to agree on a deposit – they're very common. If they really push back on it, that could be a red flag that they aren't committed.

If they do agree on a deposit, the buyer needs to place it in escrow as soon as the LOI is signed – then you can move to due diligence once the funds are secured. That deposit is like collateral for the fact that you've accepted their offer, aren't entertaining other inquiries, and are starting to share deep details about the company in the due diligence phase.

Negotiations

Remember, it's incredibly uncommon that an LOI will come in that you immediately accept and sign your name on the agreement.

*An exception here is if you provided them with the LOI template, and all they entered is the purchase price in the amount you want – in that case, accept and sign that LOI, ASAP, to move it along.

But if they drafted it themselves and added things that the two of you haven't agreed on yet, there's naturally some back-and-forth on everything from price, terms, provisions, where the funds are coming from, timing of the release of funds, deposits, and more.

If you do not fully understand the terms they are presenting, then definitely get your lawyer involved briefly before signing.

By the time they submit an LOI, it shouldn't be the first time you are discussing most of these points with the buyer. You should have already chatted about what price range is fair, what types of capital they have access to, and what closing timeframe they expect. This is always best done face-to-face, ideally in person, if not on Zoom, then phone.

Stock vs. Asset Sale

These are the two main ways a business acquisition can be structured. It can definitely get complicated, so we don't want to dig too deep into here, however, this is where it's beneficial to get your CPA and lawyer involved because there are distinct tax implications between the two. A stock sale is often the approach taken for small businesses, and it is generally simpler to execute. An M&A attorney can help you out with how to properly legally structure the deal.

Seller Financing

It's common that a buyer presents their offer with different sources of funding: maybe 90% of the purchase price from a loan (SBA or private) and the remaining 10% as seller financing.

As we talked about at the beginning of this chapter, seller financing means you don't get that money upfront – you are acting as the bank. You'd be the one carrying some of the purchase price for the buyer as a loan, with an established repayment rate and terms. These come up often and aren't an automatic red flag – in fact, they can be a great way to get the price you want. Remember, we don't recommend carrying more than 20% *maximum* as seller financing (if any).

Creative Financing

Depending on the size of your business, you might have more complicated deal terms presented in the offer. This becomes more common as the purchase price increases. It could include a combination of any of the following: seller financing, equity, stock or shares in the acquiring parent company, earnouts, etc. This is where you want to involve a lawyer who specializes in M&A. Personally, this is what I love about dealmaking. There are a million different ways to structure a deal.

Working Capital

Sometimes your buyer will request that you leave working capital in the business. They want to make sure there are funds in the company accounts to cover the monthly expenses, instead of having to pull that out of their pocket on top of the purchase price they just paid. Usually, one or two months' worth of working capital is standard to ensure that the business can continue daily operations. The buyer can also adjust the purchase price based on the working capital at the time of the sale.

Like everything, this is negotiable. Since it has been such a sellers' market lately, we've seen less working capital requirements from buyers (only once in the past several deals). Also, keep in mind that if the buyer is getting an SBA loan, it's possible for the loan to allocate extra for working capital.

Loans 101

It's common that a buyer will pay for the business with a loan – sometimes they come up with a portion of cash, other times it is fully loan funded.

SBA Loans

Breakdown: One of the most popular types of public loans used for acquisitions are SBA loans. The SBA (Small Business Administration) is a US government agency that provides support to businesses through different loan programs. The name might throw you off: SBA loans can be used for medium businesses too. A small portion of seller financing is not uncommon with SBA loans.

Remember: the SBA doesn't fund the loan directly; they approve the loan for third-party lenders to service. Think of this as similar to buying a house.

Qualifications: For an SBA loan to get approved for funding, a few things must qualify:

- Your business has to qualify for the purchase price that the buyer has agreed to (aka a fair market valuation). This will be based on the historical P&Ls, balance sheets, and (importantly) tax returns that you'll provide the buyer to submit. The business needs to have enough profit to service the loan. There will be a formal 3rd party appraisal done during underwriting, so if your business is overpriced the buyer will need to come up with the difference or you'll have to unfortunately lower the price.

- The buyer's financial standing – even if your business qualifies for the loan based on its own financials, if the buyer is in poor financial standing, it may get denied on their end. A solid credit score of at least 700, consistent income, and other assets that they own, all contribute to servicing the loan.

- The buyer needs cash for the down payment: Usually they need to put down between 10% and 20% of the total loan amount.

- The buyer needs to articulate how they will be using the loan. The SBA requires that the buyer has at least two years of industry experience in the same industry so they can carry on the business successfully.

*If a buyer has done the work of getting pre-qualified, the SBA usually gives soft approval on prequalification. They tend to go low with the pre-qual number to be safe, because they want it to go through.

There *are* other factors that could impact the ability for a business to get SBA approval. Digital businesses are slightly tougher, but still achievable, because they don't have physical assets. If your business is digital, the asset is considered goodwill. Newer businesses are also tougher to qualify – the longer your business has been in operation, the better. Even better if it's on an upward trajectory (I know, broken record) because the SBA sees it as easier for the loan to be paid off with growing revenues.

Buyers like SBA loans because they often come with lower down payments, longer repayment terms, and more flexible requirements than many other lending options. But, on your end, the prolonged application process can be a nail-biter.

Timeline: There are plenty of upsides of going the SBA route, but one warning is that it can be a lengthy process. They ballpark it anywhere from 60 to 90 days (in our personal experience, I've seen plenty of times that it's moved much faster though). This timeline is partially because it's a government agency, so they're often on their own clock, but also they are very detailed with their review of the application. They really want to mitigate risk, so they like to see a very healthy financial status and business plan to make sure the borrower and the business are capable of servicing the loan. They have only a 2% failure rate on these loans so for a buyer they have a 98% success rate if they acquired your business with an SBA loan which is amazing odds. Every seller wants to make sure their business continues on.

Private Loans

Breakdown: Private loans, on the other hand, are typically sourced from non-bank entities, like private lenders or individual investors, and aren't guaranteed by the government. These lenders might be focused on specific industries or business stages. They can have higher rates and repayment terms for buyers because that lender is taking more of a risk.

Qualifications: The requested materials to qualify for the loan will be similar as SBA, but the lender may be more flexible.

- Collateral: The buyer may need to have tangible assets or alternative forms of collateral.

- Creditworthiness: The buyer needs to have a healthy credit score for the lender to consider it serviceable, but the threshold might be more lenient compared to traditional government loans.
- Business Plan: The buyer should show the viability and profitability of the business being acquired (so the lender knows they'll get their money back).

Timeline: Unsurprisingly, it's common that private loans can be secured more swiftly because the government isn't directly involved as an essential loan step. Depending on the lender and the complexity of the deal, funds can sometimes be accessible within a few weeks or even days. But these can come at a cost: an expedited process might mean higher rates and stricter repayment terms.

Whichever loan you go with, the buyer should specify on the LOI how they plan to finance the purchase. Once you accept the LOI, this loan process actually begins. A loan can be pre-approved on your end, based on the health of the business, but it will always require that buyer's portion of the application for it to move forward.

TIP:

Sometimes, when you've accepted an LOI and are moving toward closing, it might not get approved for the full purchase price you agreed on.

Don't freak out. The deal can still go through.

It's rare that the entire loan gets rejected, unless there are some glaring issues, but it may be approved for less than expected. (For example: you agreed and signed an LOI for $1.5M but it appraised for $1.2M). Like mentioned earlier, this means the buyer has to come up with the cash elsewhere or you have to accept that lower price.

Don't settle for that lower price.

Buyers have lots of options to secure the extra cash to make up the difference. And if they really don't have any access to funds to make up a small difference, consider: do you really want them buying your company if they're that low on cash?

If the buyer calls you up trying to renegotiate the deal because the appraisal came in lower, some of their options to come up with the rest of the funds include:
- Private lenders

> - Rolling funds out of a 401K (if the buyer has ever had a corporate job)
> - Pulling funds out if home equity (if the buyer owns property)
> - Loans from investors, friends, family
>
> **Get creative together. You deserve the price you agreed on.**

Leveraging Offers

Ideally at this stage, more than one offer is coming in. This is the benefit of setting an offer date: you are more likely to get multiple LOIs at the same time so you can compare them directly, and the buyers know that other offers are on the table.

When faced with several LOIs from eager buyers, your initial impulse may be to gravitate towards the highest bid. But a lot of times, the best deal is found in the nuances. Details like payment structure, the source of funds, whether they're offering a deposit, whether they're prequalified, and your gut feeling about the buyer all matter. You shouldn't just be looking at price, you should be looking at the *likelihood of closing*.

I like to say that **having multiple offers on the table is *not* like comparing offers apples to apples.** It's more like comparing apples to carrots to candy bars. They are usually structured in such different ways that it requires nuance to decipher which is best for your unique needs.

For example, maybe one offer is 10% higher, but it's SBA financed, and they also want you to carry $80,000 of the remaining price. There's some risk here, because they don't have as much cash to work with, so if the approval doesn't come in for that amount, the deal could fall apart. If there's another offer on the table at a lower price but more or entirely cash, it could be worth going that direction – especially if their projected close date is sooner with a simpler Due Diligence phase. Again, *likelihood of closing* is one of the most important factors in deciding which offer to accept.

But luckily, if you have more than one offer on the table, you can leverage them against each other. In this case, if there's a buyer who you like more and think is a better fit, but their offer isn't as high, you can tell them that you have another one on the table for *X* amount (whatever that other offer is for). Tell them that you want to go with their offer, but you have a higher one in play – if they can match that price, you'd love to make it happen.

Agreeing & Signing the LOI
When the terms are clear and everyone's on the same page, it's

time to sign the LOI. Review the whole thing one last time, ensure everything lines up with what you agreed on, and if you want, have your legal counsel give it a once-over.

Remember, this isn't the endgame. LOIs are meant to be fairly simple, not 50 pages. The longest one we have seen is just 4 pages. The LOI is the blueprint, it's the framework on which the acquisition is built. It's an initial commitment, yes, but it's also a test of seriousness.

LOIs can be signed digitally; it's rare that a buyer will want a 'wet signature' on this (although sometimes a physical signature is requested for the Purchase Agreement, but we'll get there).

Chapter 7:
Close & Transfer

"Time kills all deals."

So, you've got the LOI signed: Celebrate, but don't pop the champagne just yet. You're about to step into the intense process of reaching the close.

First, let's talk about **deal fatigue**. It is a real thing.

This is where you get worn down by the selling process – and it starts hitting hard when you are deep into Due Diligence. It feels like having to do your taxes, but twice as hard and time consuming. You're getting tired, stressed, running on fumes. Meanwhile, you're still running your company. It's a very vulnerable time for you. This is when the buyer might try to "re-trade".

Re-trading (How to Avoid at All Costs)

What does re-trading mean?

This is when a buyer tells you they are now going to pay less for the company than you initially agreed on, or they change some other terms in their favor.

Of course, this is usually done towards the end (sometimes even the day before closing) of the transaction. At this point, you have so much riding on the sale and you're counting down the minutes until you hand it off – buyers know this, and they know you can't imagine starting again from square one.

You've probably already spent the money in your head, or maybe even racked up some credit card debt figuring you can easily pay it off once your deal closes. Because of the timing, it's common for sellers to give in due to the pressure and the desire to just be done with the deal.

You have to stay strong. You have to be willing to walk away. More than likely, they are bluffing to see if they can get away with paying less. Obviously, if the revenue of your business has decreased since the deal went under contract (maybe you lost a big client, or a key employee), then of course this can be a reasonable solution, especially if the buyer is really about to walk.

Here's a tip on how to prevent this. It's played a role in why I have not had a single re-trade happen to either my own deal or my client's deals:

- Manage the expectation at the beginning. Tell them confidently and politely when you accept their LOI that re-trading is not an option during the transaction. You are sticking to this offer and they will need to do the same.

- Mention that it's a great company so you will be willing to walk away if they attempt to re-trade. A lot of sellers are afraid to bring this up – they think that by mentioning it at the beginning, they are planting it in the buyer's head or manifesting the unwanted. But this makes a big difference in heading off any risky business. Best to find out sooner than later if they're that type of buyer. It makes you look legit – not like a pushover.

Due Diligence

Once the LOI is signed, you'll enter a phase called Due Diligence (DD).

This is when the buyer pores through the details of your business. DD is an intense examination phase by the buyer before finalizing a deal – essentially a deep dive into your business's inner workings. They're looking for any potential skeletons in the closet (legal issues, financial discrepancies, etc.) that could impact the value or long-term viability of the business.

In essence, DD is the rigorous examination your buyer conducts to ensure they're getting what they bargained for. This phase is critical. It's where many deals fall apart if not handled properly.

They'll hit you with a lot of requests for information and materials. If they're purchasing the company with a loan, many of the requested documents will be for loan approval (usually lots of financial reports to make sure they can service the loan based on the company's cash flow). Make sure you have all your documentation, financials, traffic analytics, intellectual property rights, contracts, and other relevant data in place and ready for review. Here's a deeper breakdown:

Financial Scrutiny
Buyers will pore over your books. We're talking 2 years of bank statements, 3 years of tax returns, profit and loss statements, balance sheets, and sales records. They'll look for inconsistencies or anomalies in revenue streams, expenses, or anything hinting at financial manipulation. Subscription model companies often need a close inspection of churn rates and customer lifetime value.

Operational Scrutiny

The buyer will want to see operational assets like SOPs, training materials, team onboarding, all the resources you use to run the business. This will include:

- Org charts
- An overview of what the day-to-day workflow looks like. Are there procedures in place, or is the business reliant on specific talents or the relationships of current staff/ownership?
- Your full tech stack (if this wasn't in the Data Room)
- Supply chains and vendor relationships (often with examples of communication) *remove names*
- Customer sales history *still keep the names private until close*

Legal Scrutiny

They also want to make sure things are safe on the legal side. A buyer will look into:

- Any ongoing or potential lawsuits
- The structure of your contracts with employees, vendors, or partners. Are there any potential liabilities or stipulations that could affect the new owner?
- Intellectual property (this is huge for digital businesses). Buyers will verify that trademarks,

copyrights, or patents are in order and fully transferable.

Do not wait to assemble these DD materials until this phase. You should already have most of them (like SOPs, patent records, tax returns, etc.) in a folder and ready to go. The buyer will have other specific requests which you can gather for them in real time.

Your role in Due Diligence is to give them what they need. This includes:

- *Being prepared:* Have all your documents organized, up-to-date, and readily accessible. This not only accelerates the process but also builds the buyer's confidence in the acquisition and your professionalism. Anticipate the questions buyers are likely to ask and have the answers ready.

- *Being honest:* Don't try to hide issues or sugarcoat the less appealing aspects of your business. Buyers appreciate transparency, and deception is a sure way to kill a deal. Any hiccups should have already been discussed pre-LOI, and, if possible, present a plan on how they can be resolved. This proactive stance helps reassure buyers.

- *Maintaining normal operations*: Keep running your business as usual. A dip in performance during due diligence can spook buyers. Continue to pursue growth and land new clients.

- *Keeping communication consistent:* Be available to clarify points and answer questions. Respond to their requests as soon as you can, and if a request is going to take you a bit to assemble, give them an ETA on it. Regular check-ins keep the process on track and keep a relationship with the buyers.

- *Slow & careful integration:* Towards the end of Due Diligence (after the loan has been approved and the deal is looking 99% done), this is when it's acceptable to let the buyer potentially speak to key employees or clients (if at all – this is also perfectly fine to do *after* closing). The beginning of DD is *too early* to do this – the risk of team members learning too soon should be avoided. You also don't want to spook any of your clients. To be on the safe side, if you must introduce them prior to closing, the buyer can present themselves as a consultant or potential investor.

Escrow, Simplified

Escrow helps act as a financial safety net. If you and the buyer agreed on a deposit, a third party holds onto the cash and distributes it when the time is right. On Closing Day, when both you and the buyer have confirmed that the PA is signed, the deposit will be released to you as part of the purchase price.

Purchase Agreements 101

You're in the home stretch. After successfully navigating DD, you'll move to the Purchase Agreement – now it's time to put pen to paper and finalize the deal. The PA is the binding contract that lays out all the terms and conditions of the sale. It's the rulebook for your exit, and you need to understand it inside and out.

This is your official contract detailing the terms of sale, covering everything from the agreed price, payment terms, potential liabilities, and more. Review it with a magnifying glass, preferably alongside a good attorney. We can refer you to some great ones if you do not already have one.

Lawyers: Good or Bad?

Speaking of lawyers, a saying in our industry is "lawyers kill deals".

I don't necessarily believe this. As an intermediary, I am mediating between my seller, the buyer, the banks, and the lawyers, so if you're running your sale on your own, just make sure to do the same. Don't let the lawyer take over all communication on your behalf. This could risk damaging your deal if you are not properly managing all parties to come to a mutual agreement.

Lawyers are there to protect their clients. They are essential and valuable in so many cases. However, I have also seen lawyers redline an entire purchase agreement so that they can go back and forth to rack up their bill, so be cautious of that. The key is finding a good one you trust, who shares your vision of the end goal.

TIP:

Let's normalize something out the gate: there will be plenty of back-and-forth with the buyer and their lawyer when it comes to PA drafting negotiations. After all, it has more provisions and details than the LOI.

There will be so many small nuances, specific words that one of you isn't comfortable with, requests, negotiations, compromises. Be prepared for several versions of the PA to be exchanged before each side signs off. This is normal.

What's not normal is getting hung up on small things so much that you hit a standstill. If it feels like this is happening, and you've been communicating about sections over email, get on a call to screen-share it and hash things out. Your lawyers should be on it too.

Common Components of a Purchase Agreement:

Legal Language (be prepared for legalese)
Purchase Agreements are dense and full of legal terminology. But don't let that intimidate you. Your job is to ensure that it reflects the deal you agreed to.

Purchase Price & Payment Terms
This sounds like a no-brainer, but be sure to confirm the purchase price is correct and clearly stated, aligning with the LOI you accepted. The closing date and transfer terms will also be inside. More importantly, break down the payment terms. How much cash is there and how is it financed? Is there a deposit? Earn-out arrangement? Seller carry? Deposit?

Representations & Warranties
These are your promises about the business's current state. Be honest, but also be smart. Limit your liabilities wherever you can. If something isn't in your control, don't warrant it.

Assets
There will likely be an exhibit at the end of the PA breaking down the full assets of the business being transferred and is usually called an "Allocation of Assets". Please run this breakdown by your CPA for advice and tax implications. This will include all

business assets, domains, intangibles, IP, patents, all that. Make sure everything is accurately listed (and if there's anything you are holding onto, it should be specified). Missed assets can mean missed value. The day the funds are transferred should be the same day the assets are transferred.

Indemnifications

Fancy word, but this is about liability. If something goes wrong post-sale, tying back to when you owned the company, how protected are you? Negotiate caps and time limits on indemnifications to protect yourself.

Covenants & Noncompetes

These are your promises for post-sale behavior. Noncompete clauses fall under this. It's standard for buyers to request noncompete terms inside the Purchase Agreement. Essentially, a noncompete means that you agree not to start or operate in a business that directly competes with the one you're selling, for a certain amount of time. Please make sure it is **very specific**.

Here's a noncompete example of a recent business we sold (an online book review membership site). The owner had a great 24+ year run with her business and was finally retiring. However, the initial proposed noncompete said she could not do anything in the writing or general book-related space for five years – way too broad and restrictive. That included if she ever wanted to maybe work at a library, bookstore, etc. Of course we dialed it in to specify that she could not start another online book review website business.

Take a good look at the scope and duration of the noncompete before signing. 24 months is common. Make sure the restrictions are reasonable depending on what you plan to do next (and make sure this is discussed with the buyer).

Termination Rights

Under what conditions can either party back out? Break these down in the PA. If they put down a deposit, that will come into play here too – specify whether it's nonrefundable. Usually deposits are nonrefundable, meaning you keep it if the buyer backed out by choice (but of course, if you misrepresented a part of the business or chose to cancel the deal yourself, it would be returned to them).

Dispute Resolution

It's not common that this situation actually happens, but any cautious lawyer will agree that this provision needs to be written into the PA to be safe: If things go south post-sale, how are disputes handled?

Arbitration? Litigation?

Lean on Your Advisors

This is where your legal team earns their keep. Have them review every line, explain every clause, and negotiate every point that's not in your favor. But, at the same time, lawyers can get caught up in the minutia and lose the big picture of coming together to make things work. Lawyers are a common reason that deals fall apart – sometimes the buyer and seller are on the same page, but the legal teams get extremely granular and things get complicated. Pick one that shares your approach, and you should be fine.

Remember Your Leverage

You have something the other party wants – your business. Don't be afraid to speak up and counter things, especially if they bring the first draft (since the person to draft it likely has things worded in their favor). A Purchase Agreement is a negotiation, not a dictation by anyone.

Read, Review, and Reflect

Once you're done going back and forth with the buyer on each part, read the agreement from start to finish, then do it again. This is a big moment, and you need to fully be on board with the terms. Make sure this deal aligns with your goals and values.

Close with Confidence

When you feel comfortable, when every term has been negotiated and every clause agreed on, it's time to sign. It's possible that either you or the buyer (or one of your lawyers) will want a 'wet signature' meaning it's manually signed and not just digitally. You can head to your closest notary service to get this done pretty quickly, then overnight the docs to the other party for signing.

Zero Out Your Balance Sheet

This is a question we get a lot: *Do I need to pay off all my debt before listing my company for sale?*

Nope. In many cases we advise against this because your company might take a while to sell and it could place unnecessary financial strain in the meantime.

Depending on the sale structure, many sellers clear off outstanding debts on the same day the sale funds are wired. Think of this similar to selling a house: you can sell a home if you still have a mortgage on it, the loans are first paid off when it's sold, and you're left with the remainder. In the business bank accounts, you'll take out any additional cash or savings and close them out. You earned that money, so it's yours. This is referred to as zeroing out your balance sheet. However, if leaving behind working capital is part of your transaction, be sure to set that aside.

Back in the day, I got a call from one of my sellers on closing day, asking me what to do with the money that was still sitting inside her cash register. Of course, she earned it before they took ownership, so I had to remind her that it was hers to keep.

Pre-paids, Gift Certificates, Memberships

These can be tricky because they fall into the category of income *collected* by you, but *fulfilled* by the new owner on their dime.

It's common for the value of pre-paids, gift certificates, and memberships to be deducted from the purchase price. This is often seen as the most straightforward way to reconcile these liabilities at closing that the buyer will inherit.

- *Pre-Paids:* These are payments received for services or goods not yet delivered. The seller (you) has effectively collected money for products or services that the buyer will have to provide in the future. The value of these pre-paids is typically deducted from the purchase price, or a separate fund is set aside from the sale proceeds for the buyer to cover these costs.
- *Gift Certificates:* Like pre-paids, gift certificates are liabilities. The buyer is responsible for honoring these

once they take over the business without seeing income for fulfilling them. The value of outstanding gift certificates is often deducted from the sale price or handled similarly to pre-paids. With a couple of my personal exits, I negotiated to pay them back to the buyer as they came in for redemption, so this could be an option too.

- *Memberships:* For businesses with membership models (like gyms or clubs), memberships sold by the seller but extending into the period after the sale are liabilities for the buyer. The approach can be similar to pre-paids and gift certificates. In some cases, these might be adjusted on a pro-rata basis. For instance, if a membership extends six months into the new ownership, half of its value might be deducted.

Remember: When it comes to these negotiations, lawyers can help determine the fair value of these liabilities and the best way to explicitly incorporate them into the purchase agreement.

Handoff on Close Day

On closing day, the funds will be transferred, and you'll officially hand off the business. This means all business accounts, logins, and platforms move over to the buyer.

Digital Assets

Make sure all logins, passwords, and access to digital assets are securely shared. This includes your hosting accounts, CMS logins, social media accounts, and all third-party services. We have a helpful **Login Transfer** spreadsheet in our resources section you can use by scanning the QR code at the end of this chapter.

Employee Transition

It's up to you when you tell your team, but usually it is on the actual day of close. Many sellers will tell their key employees or managers sooner, but this should only be done when the close is 100% confirmed, on the off chance that something falls through.

Email Transfer

As the owner, you probably have a personal email tied to the business account. So what do you do if you have a **YourName@YourCompany.com** email address?

You have two options:

(1) See if the buyer will let you keep it and do a temporary auto-forward until you are able to get everything switched over. After a few months, they can delete your email account without things falling through the cracks.

(2) The owner might want to take it over and just forward emails that pertain specifically to you.

After learning this lesson a few times the hard way, I now use a company specific email that can easily be handed off to the new owner without issues (Relax@SpaEcoChateau.com, Exit@TheMagnoliaFirm.co). It's why I don't have Christine@TheMagnoliaFirm.co

Training

No doubt your buyer is smart, but they don't know the intricacies of your business like you yet. It's common to offer a transition period, where you guide them through operations and other nuances.   Transferring a digital business isn't like handing over the keys to a car. It's a complex process, with multiple elements needing to be transitioned smoothly to ensure the continued success of the business.

Customer and Client Transition

Personal introductions and a transition plan for key customers or clients can help preserve the business's value. Your buyer might be great at business, but you've built relationships they have yet to establish. Remember: your customer contracts or employee contracts may have to be re-signed if they aren't transferable. It's best for the buyer to knock these out as soon as they take over.

Post-Sale Training

We covered my story with this in Chapter One, so now let's tie it all in. Sellers usually agree to a period of training for the new owner (outlined in the purchase agreement). You and the buyer should have clear written boundaries of what this will entail. These training sessions can be crucial for maintaining the business's value – especially if there is an earnout component to the deal, because your remaining chunk of cash depends on how the business performs in their hands. Regardless of whether you have an earnout, you want to set them up for success. Every detail about the transfer process should be documented – this includes responsibilities, timelines, and contingencies. It's not just red tape; it's your safety net. The more processes are documented, the less training you have to do because the buyer can refer back to those resources instead of pulling in your time. You can offer an hourly consulting rate for any support needed beyond the training terms. However, don't be unreasonable and nickel-and-dime the new owner if they have occasional questions. This business is your baby, you want it to succeed, *and* you were paid a good chunk of money – so always respond and be willing to answer simple questions if the buyer contacts you in the future. For most of my exits, they usually reach out a few times up to two years post-transaction, which I am always fine with and do not charge for. Plus, it's always nice to get an update on how the business is doing.

TIP:

Stay in contact with the buyer and be available if they have quick questions down the road.

You want the business to succeed in their hands.

Another benefit of keeping in touch (if you're open to this) is you can let the buyer know that if they are having a hard time running the business, or if they ever want to move on from it, to contact you first. You might be willing to take it back over (at a good deal of course)!

Announcing the Sale

Once the business has passed into the buyer's hands, it's up to the two of you how publicly you want to be about the acquisition. Some owners do a social media announcement, others, just share it via email to their database, others choose to keep quiet and only share with each client that needs to know. This will depend on the company, industry, and of course what you and the buyer want to do.

Don't Forget About Taxes & Other Fees

Here's the not-so-fun part. Yep, you get taxed on the sale proceeds.

Upon the sale of your business, expect to set aside **at least** 30% of the sale funds for capital gains taxes. And remember, this percentage might be higher or lower depending on your jurisdiction. The exact tax rate will vary based on where you live (if you live in California like me, it's even higher than 30%, in other states it can be quite a bit lower). But, before you groan at the tax bite, there's hope. As our golden rule: Always overestimate, so you're not caught short.

TIP:

Reach out to a Wealth Advisor in advance for tax-saving strategies.

Ideally, the best time to do this is at the **very beginning of listing your business** because you can work backwards to determine the purchase price you're willing to accept.

If you're working with a broker, you also need to subtract their fee from the bottom line to gauge what amount you'll walk away with (but lucky for you, if you're reading this book, you're probably selling on your own which skips those fees).

If the sale is over \$1M, consider using a wealth manager to set up a trust. Most people think it only applies to much larger sums of cash – but even at this size it can really benefit you.

My good friend did this when she sold her business: by placing the funds in a trust, she was able to reduce the taxable amount and create an investment vehicle where the trust pays her monthly.

It's your call whether you want to pocket the full sale amount upfront or get creative with financial strategies.

Your risk tolerance plays a big role here. When the market is good, this can pay off. I have friends getting a 10% return on their money: let's say you sold for \$12 million, you pay taxes on the \$2 million that you decide to keep (capital gains can range anywhere from 25-40% based on where you live). The remaining \$10 million goes into a trust giving you monthly cash flow, which at 10%, you can do the math. Not bad right?

Of course, I'm just giving a birds-eye overview here because this book is about how to *sell* your business, and post-sale is a strategy all its own that a financial expert can go deep with you on. But I wanted to include this part so you know that there are creative ways to shelter your money once the deal closes.

Free resources from this chapter:

To access all the guides includes the Transfer Spreadsheet and more, you can *scan the code here:*

Conclusion

At this point we've gone on a journey together.

We started with the *idea* of selling, exploring the serious benefits that come with exiting your business.

We walked through how to strategize your exit, organize your financials, list your business, and talk to interested buyers.

We broke down LOIs, Purchase Agreements, Due Diligence and post-close steps.

You now know just as much, if not more, than a lot of brokers out there. You have the tools to cash out and move forward to whatever comes next.

This is where you ask yourself: *What do I want my life to look like now? How does selling my business move me into that reality?*

You've worked hard building an asset. Now, you've got a golden ticket to capitalize on. But let's be real – it's not just about the money. It's about what the money can do for you. It's about the freedom it brings. Imagine waking up every day knowing you can do whatever you want, whenever you want, however you want. That's a reality you can create here.

Sure, I wrote this book to share the tactical steps of selling, but on a deeper level we wanted to bring about a **shift in perspective**. By simplifying this 'confusing' concept of selling a company, the goal is to change beliefs about what's possible. Selling your company, with or without help, is completely possible.

Use this opportunity to re-architect your life.
When you're ready to sell, each section will be here for you. I know you can do it.

Free Bonus Resources:

To access all the guides in this book, you can *scan the code here:*

About the Authors

Christine McDannell is the Principal and Lead Business Intermediary of **The Magnolia Firm**, a boutique M&A brokerage firm specifically serving digital/online businesses. They help business owners achieve the perfect exit in record time by using tech, AI, and automations to get the job done.

After founding, growing, and selling 20+ of her own businesses across diverse verticals including house cleaning, wellness, beauty, real estate, and a successful tech exit in 2021, Christine realized that there was a formula behind the perfect business exit and now dedicates her full-time attention to helping others do the same.

She is passionate about all things business, especially helping entrepreneurs step into the next phase of life with their dream business exit.

In her free time, you can catch her at live music festivals, spontaneous travel spots around the world, attending Burning Man, or playing Boat Captain in the beautiful San Diego Bay.

Lauren Mauldwin is a Business Intermediary and Exit Advisor specializing in privately owned SMBs. After graduating at the top of her class from Loyola Marymount University, she had several stints in early and mid-stage startups, plus a few business ventures of her own in the wellness and service industries, until bringing it all together in the M&A space.

At first, her initial impression breaking into the industry was a lot of *"Wait, what? Why are brokers doing it this way?"*

And most of the time, the widespread response was something like *"Well, we don't know... that's kind of just how it's always been."*

The process seemed outdated — detached from the needs of innovative business owners looking for guidance to sell their life's work. With this in mind, Lauren focuses on integrating new tech into the M&A process to carve a more efficient path to the finish line, making space for a client-centered approach personalized to their needs.

When she's not reviewing P&Ls, Lauren loves coastal hikes, testing new pasta recipes, learning chords on her new guitar (badly), and stealing quality time with her friend's dogs.

Disclaimer:

No part of this book may be reproduced without written permission by the author. The information provided in this book is for general informational purposes only. The methods described are not intended to be a definitive set of instructions. Reading this book does not create a client relationship between us. This content is not intended to be a source of financial or legal advice. It should not be used as a substitute for the personal advice of a competent professional equipped with details about your specific company and situation.

The author(s) and the publisher make no guarantee of financial results obtained by using this book. The goal of this material is to provide educational and informational resources that are intended to help you succeed in selling your business. Your ultimate success or failure will be the result of your own efforts, your particular situation, and innumerable other circumstances beyond the authors' knowledge and control.